The
Garland Library
of
War and Peace

The
Garland Library
of
War and Peace

Under the General Editorship of

Blanche Wiesen Cook, *John Jay College, C.U.N.Y.*

Sandi E. Cooper, *Richmond College, C.U.N.Y.*

Charles Chatfield, *Wittenberg University*

Realistic Pacifism

The Ethics of War
and
The Politics of Peace

by

Leyton Richards

with a new introduction
for the Garland Edition by
Charles Chatfield

Garland Publishing, Inc., New York & London
1972

Library of Congress Cataloging in Publication Data

Richards, Leyton Price, 1879-1948.
    Realistic pacifism.

    (The Garland library of war and peace)
    "This book combines into a single volume two
separate books which were published in England, the one
in 1929 and the other in 1935. They bore the titles
respectively, The Christian's alternative to war and
The Christian's contributions to peace."
    1. War and religion. 2. Peace. 3. Nationalism.
4. Pacifism. I. Title. II. Series.
JX1952.R47 1972   327'.172   79-147676
ISBN 0-8240-0433-7

Introduction

Written in the lucid prose of one of modern Britain's great preachers, this book is a clear exposition of recent Christian pacifism in relation to international war. It is a case for a form of pacifism that would be reasonable, willing to make distinctions about political reality. It is neither theological nor historical, although Richards was well versed in the theological and historical studies of Christian pacifism being made by his colleagues Charles Raven and Cecil Cadoux, among others. Rather, it is a common sense view of the matter.

Richards rested his case upon a series of distinctions. First, and in common with a number of pacifist thinkers interpreting World War I, he distinguished between coercive force, which under some circumstances is essential and legitimate for society, and warfare, which is a particular and anti-social use of force. Second, he distinguished the purpose or sanction of warfare, which may be moral in intent, from the method of war which, he argued, overcomes only enemies and not evil — since warfare itself is the evil and the challenge for modern mankind.

Third, he distinguished between the ethics appropriate to the personal life of the confessed

INTRODUCTION

Christian who has pledged his commitment to the way of Jesus and, on the other hand, the choices open to peoples not under the universal authority of Christian values. This, in turn, enabled Richards to distinguish the actions appropriate for Christians as individuals — conscientious objection to war service, for example — from those actions appropriate to them as citizens — strengthening international organization and combatting the ideology of exclusive state sovereignty.

The book is organized around these distinctions and a few others, and it remains today as cogent as the day it was published. In important respects it anticipated and countered the ethical objections to pacifism that have been raised by Reinhold Niebuhr and some other theologians searching for realism in the midst of international dilemmas.

The greatest weakness of the book is that Richards did not adequately distinguish the traditions of nationalism and militarism from the power relationships they express and fortify. For this reason his book, however realistic, is incomplete. But if it does not outline the search for an equitable distribution of power that must, in the last analysis, accompany any significant development of internationalism, it does establish the importance and example of clear, reasonable, and relative analysis of public choices for pacifists and nonpacifists alike. In this regard, it marks a significant development of thought by those who would transcend the claims of national *sovereignty in the interest of peace; and it also is representative of the life and thought of its author.*

He was born in 1879 into the modest household of an accountant in Sheffield, England; but hard times led his family to emigrate to the United States. Richards was nine then and, although his family returned to England after about two years, his American experience impressed him greatly. He subsequently made over two score transatlantic crossings, and both his memories of nationalism in the American school room and his confidence in federal republican forms of government found their way into Realistic Pacifism.

With the help of tutoring from his minister and special work at Gordons College, Aberdeen, Richards met the terms for admission to Glasgow University, and he earned his M.A. there in preparation for the Congregational ministry. There, too, he earned an enduring reputation for skill in oratory and debate and for liberal politics, and he broadened his world outlook by working on tramp steamers in the long vacation periods – of necessity for he had to support himself. He completed his studies with three years at Mansfield College, Oxford. Richards had preached from time to time in Peterhead during his college years, and he was called there to succeed the regular minister. After about a year he was married to Edith Ryley. Not only was she a source of quiet strength throughout his life, but she recorded Richards' story in her Private View of a Public Man *(London, 1950), the source of most of our knowledge about him.*

In 1911 they sailed to Melbourne, then the seat of the Commonwealth Government, where Leyton Richards had accepted the pastorate of the large Collins Street Independent Church. His long-standing liberal political views were reawakened in response to the obligations of religious leadership, initially with respect to the White Australia policy of excluding non-white immigrants which he opposed as it affected individuals, but most significantly with regard to conscription.

It was peacetime still, but the Commonwealth government had passed a conscription law providing for military training beginning at the age of twelve and for reserve status until the age of sixty. Exemption was provided for religious objectors, notably Quakers, but the burden of proof fell upon the objector — even at the age of twelve — and exemption was extended only to combat duties. This threat to rights of conscience aroused Richards, who spoke against the act from the pulpit. Immediately he was placed in the center of the controversy. When the family returned to England early in 1914, for reasons unconnected with this issue, Richards had come into close contact with Quakers and had formed definite convictions against conscription on religious grounds, opinions which preceded him to England.

He opposed Britain's entry into war, and from his new pastorate near Manchester he opposed conscription, although he defended and served the men who

8

accepted it or volunteered. For himself he could not reconcile loyalty to Jesus Christ with service in war, and he said so in and out of his pulpit. To speak his heart examined was, after all, his religious calling; and his congregation was torn between its loyalty to that conception of Congregational polity and its loyalty to the national cause. When in 1916 he was brought to trial with others who openly had opposed conscription, and was sentenced, his deacons paid the £100 fine. Nonetheless, the strain in the church was telling, and Richards offered his resignation. This was refused, but he was given a leave of absence.

Richards was a founding member of the No-Conscription Fellowship and he drew sustenance from the Christian pacifist Fellowship of Reconciliation. He participated in its relief work and he counseled conscientious objectors. For a few months he filled the pulpit at Pilgrim Church, Brooklyn, New York, and he opposed war and conscription in America as he had done at home. Upon his return to England he became General Secretary of the Fellowship of Reconciliation, with headquarters in London. Harassed by the government, proscribed from preaching in many churches, Richards still longed for a congregation of his own, and so in 1918 he accepted a call from the remarkably activist and largely pacifist Pembrook Chapel, Liverpool. Ironically, the courageous souls of this church found Richards' emphasis on Jesus too orthodox for them. The relationship was terminated, in any case, when

9

shortly after the war Richards was called back to Bowden Downs at Manchester. It was a vote of faith in him and in the unity of the Church, and he accepted.

Richards' second Bowden ministry was fruitful, and it led to his appointment in 1924 to the 1,200 member, prestigious church of Carrs Lane, Birmingham. He is best remembered for that long ministry. Even when he resigned in 1938, owing largely to throat trouble which persisted throughout his life, he served the church intermittently into World War II.

Over many years, Richards had gravitated toward Quakerism. His contacts with the Society of Friends in England and America were many. His own conception of vocation changed as with fruitful lecture tours, on one hand, and continuing throat trouble, on the other, he came to question the efficacy of preaching – always the heart of his ministry. Besides, he increasingly viewed the sacraments as expendable symbols of an inward relationship with God. It was a natural step, therefore, to a Fellowship and eventual Wardenship at Woodbrooke, the Quaker International College near Birmingham. There, from 1939 throughout the war, he was a minister without collar. In 1946 he joined the Society of Friends.

Two years after a heart attack curtailed his activity in 1945, Richards and his wife left Birmingham for Berkshire, where he died in 1948.

Richard's Realistic Pacifism *reflects his continued*

INTRODUCTION

contact with an international community of pacifists whose concerns extended beyond individual witness to the problems of social justice and world peace. He had been present in October, 1919, at the founding conference of the International Fellowship of Reconciliation at Biltoven, Holland, along with others who hoped to fashion a realistic pacifism — leaders such as F. Siegmund-Schültze from Germany, Pierre Cérésole from Switzerland, Mathilda Wrede from Finland, and Henry Hodgkin from England. Not content only to theorize about peace and to protest against war, they sought concrete steps which ordinary people could take to replace international anarchy with a universal religion. That is the point of Richards' Realistic Pacifism. With his pacifist friends he shared a dedication to what he called the "pressure of political fact. . . . establishing, in times of public indifference and by the conscious forethought of idealists, conditions which will become part of the accepted tradition of national life, and which therefore in times of national excitement will — by the very inertia of tradition — assist the maintenance of peace."

This role would not seem very realistic to critics under the stress of war, not very effective in the view of those who had, or aspired to have, political influence. But perhaps it is the common sense view of the matter for common people in times when the public is attending to domestic issues and both prowar and antiwar movements subside. It was

INTRODUCTION

typical of Richards that he should build a book upon a distinction between ethics in wartime and politics in peacetime — perhaps it was the preacher in him. Such distinctions are the heart of realism.

Charles Chatfield
Wittenberg University

REALISTIC PACIFISM

REALISTIC PACIFISM

THE ETHICS OF WAR
AND
THE POLITICS OF PEACE

BY

LEYTON RICHARDS

WILLETT, CLARK & COMPANY
CHICAGO   NEW YORK
1935

To

MY AMERICAN AND BRITISH FRIENDS
IN THE PEACE MOVEMENT

PREFACE

THIS book combines into a single volume two separate books which were published in England, the one in 1929 and the other in 1935. They bore the titles respectively, "The Christian's Alternative to War" and "The Christian's Contribution to Peace." A small edition of the former was imported into the United States under its British title, but the latter is published in America for the first time in this present volume.

The book is written from the standpoint of Christian pacifism, but at the same time the approach to the problem of world peace which is advocated in these pages is not one which can be adopted only by the Christian pacifist. There is a wide area which is occupied in common by pacifist and non-pacifist alike, and it seems to me of the utmost importance that these two shall work together and form a common public opinion wherever possible. This standpoint has governed my consideration of the various aspects of the subject, and especially my treatment of the sanctions of international peace. To many Christian pacifists the idea of a so-called international police force is anathema; but to others it is a necessary step in the final elimination of armed force from civilized intercourse; in any case, however, it is rapidly moving into the realm of practical politics, and for that reason I have devoted a chapter to its consideration in the endeavor to clear away certain misconceptions.

If in the eyes of some I seem to condemn the way of war too strongly, I can only plead that my peace convictions are built not only upon theory but upon experience; for in a way not given to many my public life for a quarter of a century has centered about the menace of militarism.

I first came against the problem as a practical issue in Australia where I had been called as minister to the Collins Street Independent Church, in the city of Melbourne; for there I found in operation a system of " boy conscription " [1] whereby every boy between the ages of twelve and fourteen was compulsorily enrolled in a cadet corps, while still at school; from fourteen to eighteen he became a " senior cadet," with the legal obligation of doing sixteen days' military drill a year; and from eighteen to twenty-six he was a member of the " citizen forces," with a further obligation to attend an annual military camp. This system of conscription was in vogue without any adequate conscience clause for the relief of those who, like the Quakers and others, feel that military service is a denial of their Christian loyalty. Consequently, the sons of these people were torn from their homes, tried in batches of fifty with

[1] This was originally introduced in 1911, but was abandoned in 1929 largely as a result of a determined and persistent agitation against it which made its continued operation both expensive and difficult. In announcing the repeal of the compulsory clauses of the Defense Act, the responsible minister stated that one of the reasons for this decision was Australia's signature of the Pact of Paris for the outlawry of war.

other delinquents, and committed to prison-forts under military control for periods of from twenty to thirty days. Moreover, this did not happen once and for all, but was repeated annually as year by year the boys refused to conform to the legal demands of the army authorities. It is only fair to say that such boys were a handful in point of numbers, but a moral principle is not invalidated because there are only a few who recognize it. What mother would like to see such things happen to her boy, whom she had trained to be a lover of peace? Then what could a Christian minister do but ask the church which he tried to serve to stand by and with her persecuted children against this oppression of Christian conscience by the state?

Later, in South Africa, I saw the graves of British soldiers which line the railway as it climbs its 5,000 feet through Natal to the high veldt at Majuba hill, and I learned something of the aftermath of bitterness which follows in the wake of war, despite the healing and courageous wisdom of the Act of Union by which South Africa became a dominion within the British empire. There on the Matoppo hills in Rhodesia was Cecil Rhodes' last resting-place, and, hard by, the memorial to Captain Wilson and his brave men ambushed in war by the Matabeles, who hated the white man — not without reason — and sought to drive him whence he came. And then, by contrast, an old man in Khama's country who loved the white man because he once had known and loved David Livingstone.

It was with this experience of the military machine,

and with this memory of the contrast between the military way and the Christian way that I touched at first hand many of the events recorded in the chapters on " The Nature of War." The impact, however, of all the desperate happenings of that nightmare period of 1914–18 merely strengthened and deepened the convictions already formed concerning war and its legitimacy from a Christian standpoint.

I have no specific acknowledgments to make for the sources of my material, apart from the footnotes at various points throughout the book; but my indebtedness to friends, known and unknown, is immense. If I have unwittingly borrowed ideas from other writers or speakers on peace and war without formal acknowledgment, I can only plead that those ideas have become so much a part of my own mind as to obscure their origin. I make no claim to originality, but only to sincere thought upon the problems of peace. In this I have been especially assisted by discussion of the subject with students and members of the faculty in various colleges of the United States and Canada, where at frequent intervals I have been privileged to give courses of lectures. This accounts for the considerable number of references to American history and affairs which occur throughout the book.

The book is offered in the hope that it may be of service in clarifying the thought of Christian people who desire to play a constructive, and not merely a negative and critical part in solving what is at once the most urgent and the most difficult public problem of the present day — the problem of insuring the peace of the world and eliminating international war from the intercourse of civilized peoples.

LEYTON RICHARDS.

BIRMINGHAM,
    ENGLAND.
        1935.

CONTENTS

INTRODUCTORY

THE Christian attitude to the issues of peace and war in the modern world is not always easy to determine, because the personal and the political elements in any given situation are often so difficult to disentangle the one from the other. In general terms, no one questions that the Christian gospel requires peace and condemns war; and the essence of the Christian case, therefore, is not merely that war is inexpedient, but that it is wrong. The opponents of war however frequently do an unwitting injustice to the case they seek to destroy; for they assume, if they do not explicitly allege, unworthy motives in the warrior. But it goes without saying that no progress can be made in mutual understanding unless there be granted at the outset full and complete recognition of the sincerity of soldier and pacifist alike: we must take both at their best and not at their worst; and the Christian objection to war, therefore, must not be confused with a condemnation of the men who felt, or who feel it their duty to fight: it ought to be possible to recognize the conscience of the fighter and his devotion to what he deems to be right while at the same time we dissent from his judgment. Oliver Cromwell's remark to the lords commissioners of the Scottish Kirk is apt in this connection for all parties to this controversy: "I beseech you, gentlemen," said Cromwell, "by the mercies of God, to deem it possible that you may be mistaken!" The institution of chattel slavery provides an analogy. No one can read *Uncle Tom's Cabin* without recognizing St. Clair, the slaveholder, as a Christian gentleman, and in him Mrs. Stowe drew for her readers a picture of the typical Southern planter of pre-abolition days: yet to the conscience of the twentieth century a Christian slaveholder is a contradiction in terms. We recognize St. Clair's sincerity in holding men as chattels, and yet without exception the churches of today negative his judgment. So in the matter of war. The only valid attitude on the part of the pacifist toward his fellow-Christians who do not share his convictions is that imputed to George Fox. On one occasion William Penn is said to have asked Fox what he should do with his sword, to which the founder of the Society of Friends replied, " Wear it so long as thou canst! " That advice still holds good. The modern world demands that we endorse the methods and the way of war as a final resort in international emergency, and in the presence of that demand the word comes to every Christian citizen: " Endorse them so long as thou canst." That is to say, so long as we can reconcile war with our Christian conscience, we have no right to repudiate the way of the sword; but, on the other hand, if from the lips and the life of Jesus Christ we learn a " more excellent way," then, in highest loyalty alike to God and to man, that better way must be the path we tread.

One other preliminary consideration needs to be set down before we proceed to deal with our problem. We need to differentiate sharply and clearly between war

and the use of force. War, of course, involves the use
of force, but — as will be shown later — it involves
other things besides; and it is these other things and not
force *per se* which gives it its distinctive quality and
character. There is no need, therefore, to confuse the
issue by setting up the Tolstoyan dilemma of either war
or nonresistance: the Christian's alternative to war may
in certain cases be an attitude of nonresistance, but on
the contrary it may not: for it is certainly never mere
sentimentalism or supine acquiescence in highhanded
wrong: peace is not a synonym for a quietist attitude to
life! Physical force — like any other gift of God to the
children of men — is in and of itself nonmoral; it is
neither good nor bad in its intrinsic quality, any more
than is any other aspect of the material world: indeed,
from the point of view of modern physics, with its
electrodynamic hypothesis, all matter is but one mani-
festation of the essential energy or force in which all
things consist. As a fact of practical everyday procedure, therefore, we can none of us dispense with the
use of force without repudiating all our contacts with
the material world; the logic of nonresistance, pressed
to its ultimate issue, is suicide; and even in that act we
must use the very force we would fain discard. But if
physical force is nonmoral, then it may be used either
for or against God's purposes. Dr. Lyman Abbott, in
his *Theology of an Evolutionist,* once put the issue
crisply, if inadequately, when he said, " Love may use
force, Hate may not "; and it is not without significance in this connection that the use of force finds a

Christian sanction in the story of the expulsion of the money-changers from the temple. The story has often been misread and misapplied by apologists for war: in Sir John Millais' well-known picture, for instance, the " scourge of small cords " becomes a cat-o'-nine-tails in the hands of Jesus, and on this basis justification has been found for all the coercive methods of modern civilization, from the loving restraint which holds an infant from harm to the hateful brutalities of the battle-field. But it is only in John's Gospel that the " scourge " is mentioned at all, and even there it is nowhere alleged that it was applied to human beings: " He drove them out of the temple, *both the sheep and the oxen,*" but apparently not the men. Also, if we take the story as it stands, it records what was obviously a triumph of moral power rather than of physical violence: grant if we will the use of Millais' " cat-o'-nine-tails," yet is it conceivable that one man thus armed could clear the temple court of its multitude of traffickers? The secret of his victory lay in the conviction which traders and people shared with Jesus that he was right and they were wrong, and it was this conviction which drove them forth rather than any coercive tactics on the part of Jesus. Nevertheless, money-changers' tables cannot be overturned without a modicum of physical force, and we may be grateful therefore that the incident has been recorded as a witness to the fact that One whose " meat was to do the will of God " found within the terms of that will a place for the use of force.

Such an admission, however, does not imply an endorsement of that specific use of physical force which we find in war. The apologist for war proves too much when he is content merely to repudiate the doctrine of nonresistance; for by a similar process of reasoning we could justify any of the hoary iniquities, from gladiatorial shows to piracy, which Christendom has long ago unanimously outlawed. War is a human institution, recognized as such by civilized peoples, definitely budgeted for and prepared for as a specific national service, and envisaged everywhere as a method adopted by human beings for dealing with certain practical emergencies in the life of nations; and while therefore the use of force may and will still have its place in the economy of civilized life, yet it is not irrational to isolate the problem of war from those other problems and practical difficulties which call for the exercise of coercive force in human relationships. The history of moral achievement suggests that organized evil is eliminated from the common life of man by a succession of attacks in detail rather than by a massed attack all along the line, and it is not therefore unduly sanguine to say that it ought to be possible to abolish the institution of war long before the Christian conscience has pronounced judgment upon all the detailed ethical questions which arise in many departments of life through the application of physical force. An analogy again may be found in the institution of chattel-slavery; for that institution was abolished in the nineteenth century, despite the fact that the prerogatives of human personality which slavery violates still await adequate

recognition in the economic and racial and other relationships of the world about us.

War and the Christian's relation to war can thus be
dealt with as a problem by itself; and as such it has two
aspects — one negative and the other positive. These
correspond roughly to the personal and the political
elements in the situation, and they underline the distinction between pacifism on the one hand and a desire
for peace on the other. Christian pacifism is a matter
of personal conviction which allows of no compromise;
those who see the will of God in Christ's reaction to
earthly evil can "do no other" than try to be faithful
to that revelation, whatever the cost to themselves or
to any worldly interest. But in the endeavor to establish international peace it may be necessary to accept
half a loaf rather than no bread at all; for in this matter
the Christian must work with others who do not share
his personal faith, and he must therefore be willing to
go with them as far as they will go with him. It is this
which so often seems to introduce an element of compromise into public policy, and which sometimes leads
Christian people to stand aloof from common effort;
but "he that is not against us is with us," and there is
no infidelity to one's ideals in welcoming a second best
where the best is beyond our grasp.

The treatment of the subject therefore at this point
falls naturally into two parts which are concerned respectively with the Christian's repudiation of war and
his contribution to the building of world peace.

PART I

PERSONAL: THE CHRISTIAN'S
REPUDIATION OF WAR

CHAPTER I

THE PROBLEM

THE late Lord Bryce declared shortly before his death that civilization must destroy war or war would destroy civilization. This fact will be considered in detail later on; but if the statement is even broadly true (and no one who knows the facts of modern warfare will question it), it means that the institution of war presents the world with a problem which is as urgent as it is grave. Indeed, unless mankind can find a substitute for war as the final court of appeal in international affairs, there will be no world to preserve and no world problems to be solved. From this point of view, therefore, the problem of the abolition of war overshadows every other problem which arises from human relationship, and it is the condition-precedent without which no final solution can be found for the social, industrial, economic, racial and other difficulties which at present engage the energies and the devotion of good men and women. The situation indeed in every country today has reached a pitch of absurdity which would destroy war and all its works in a shout of popular derision, were it not for the obsessions and fears which still hold men in bondage to their baser selves; for the endeavor to preserve civilization by means which inevitably spell its destruction reminds one of the lament of the old

9

lady who found herself compelled to " kill her cat to save it from dying! "

But if war is thus the supreme problem for the citizen, it is still more so for the Christian. For while he shares the dilemma of the citizen who is called to preserve his country by preparing for its destruction, he is also acutely conscious of a moral dilemma; for he is discovering that the Person of Jesus Christ has a relation to the fact of war, as he has to all the other facts of life. This twentieth century indeed is in some respects more definitely alive to the significance of Jesus than any century has been since the first: the cry, " Back to Jesus," which was raised in the latter decades of the nineteenth century, is bearing fruit, and through consecrated scholarship we have today a clearer conception of his relation both to God and to man than our fathers had; we understand too, as they did not, something of his relation to the wider problems of his own day: for the whole of his earthly ministry was intimately associated with the politics of the ancient world, and in his own Person he had to face the problem of participation in war. Should he follow his chosen path of fidelity to God to the bitter end? or should he succumb to Jewish expectations and construe his messiahship in terms of a military captaincy? What of Rome and its legions? The occupation of his native land by an alien and a pagan tyranny? Should he " cast out Satan by Beelzebub, the prince of the devils " and overcome the Roman arms by arming his followers? None can doubt that, with his dominant and dominating personality, he could have made a bid for political power and rallied his countrymen in the effort to drive Rome into the sea. Then why did he not do so? For centuries the ethical significance of Jesus' attitude was obscured, and he tended to become a mythological Figure involved in the toils of theological speculation: but modern scholarship has rescued him and set him once more in the midst of the world he came to save. So the Christian of today, as he faces an armed and embattled world, is asking what is the mind of Christ on this question of war; and hence the dilemma.

This dilemma has sometimes been put as " Christ or Cæsar "; but it is more subtle than that. Jesus himself found it possible to " pay tribute to Cæsar," and there are evidences both in the Gospels and in the New Testament generally that the Roman government was by no means or in every respect at variance with a true Christian faith: it stood for justice and tolerance and a wide measure of liberty between man and man, and these are Christian values. But at bottom, Rome was coercive in its government of the provinces, and the Christian of the first century had to ask himself the same question which is challenging the conscience of the Christian today.[1] In view then both of our more intimate understanding of Jesus and of the pressure of the war system upon modern life, the question cannot be burked: Is war as we know it an activity in which the Christian can be faithful to Christ or an enterprise

---

[1] For a scholarly elucidation of the problem as it confronted the first-century Christian, see C. J. Cadoux's *The Early Christian Attitude to War.*

which the church can endorse in his name? However exalted the purpose which impels men to arms, are the processes of war ever an expression of the Christian spirit or congruous with the redemptive passion which took Jesus to the cross?

If so, of course no difficulty ensues. But if not, then a question of personal responsibility emerges for everyone who is engaged directly or indirectly in the operations of war, namely this: ought I to identify my will and action with the state at war? or am I not bound — within the limits of that restricted liberty which a warring state allows me — to express Christ's will and manifest his spirit as the one and only means by which I can further his redemptive purpose in the world? It is to be noted — as will be emphasized later — that a sub-Christian world may know no better way than war for the settlement of international conflict: it is often the only way in which such a world can register its moral protest against the onslaught of evil: but is the church or the Christian man to accept on demand the way of a sub-Christian world or to be true to the will and way of Jesus Christ at any cost and at any risk of material distress to self or to others?

The common conscience of mankind does not answer these questions as it would have done even five or six decades ago: for today we have learned to distinguish between wars of aggression and wars of defense: the distinction is one which statesmen find it difficult to define, since an apparently aggressive blow may actually be struck in defense or to anticipate an attack:

also aggression may be expressed diplomatically or by policy until a neighbor people is thereby provoked into military aggression in defense — so it appears and is argued — of threatened interests. But it nevertheless registers a moral advance on the part of the modern world that wars of aggression — in the abstract at least — are never justified. Even a people or a government motived by aggressive designs always disguises its motive under a nobler name: in actual practice the plea of " defense " is usually raised, and an astute statesman can generally present his case in this guise to the people of his own country: it may be defense of one's native land, of some neighbor nation, of liberty, the weak, the persecuted, or some idealistic or moral end, of civilization, or even of Christianity. It is significant that during the World War not a single one of the belligerents admitted aggressive purposes, and one and all were anxious to impress upon public opinion in neutral countries that their side was fighting in " defense "! A curious and contradictory situation in which no one was an aggressor and all were fighting on the defensive! But it means that in the world today war can never secure popular support unless it be represented as a method of repelling and defeating the assault of evil; and it is only on such grounds that good men can be induced to engage in the operations of war as in a Christian crusade.

If the problem of war were a simple matter of either doing or not doing certain things, it would be easy to give a plain yes or no to the question of its legitimacy from a Christian standpoint; but for the individual, the problem is complicated and confused by all manner of secondary issues. For instance, the element of personal responsibility and personal decision — which is central to the Christian ethic — seems often entirely foreign to questions of war and peace: nations go to war, not private individuals, and personal responsibility therefore seems lost in the demand of the state upon its citizens whenever there comes a call to arms. Then again, when the plea of defense is raised, it seems as though we can only repudiate war by repudiating the Christian duty of succoring the needy: a Christian man, it is said, would not feel called to stand by, inert and helpless, while a bully assaulted a little child; then — however distasteful or abhorrent the clash of battle may be to our Christian sensibilities — can we refuse to act when both aggressor and victim are not individuals but nations? The problem is sometimes stated as a choice of evils from one or other of which there is no escape: thus, it may be admitted that war is not to be reconciled with the gospel of Jesus Christ, but then, so it is said, neither is a refusal to go to war (granted that we take war at its best as an endeavor to repel the assault of evil upon the community): the individual therefore has no option but to choose the lesser of two evils and stand in with his country in resisting the aggressor by the only immediately practicable means, which is the method of war. Incidentally, we may note that such a plea assumes without warrant and certainly without proof that in the presence of such a dilemma war is of necessity the lesser of two evils. In view of what has already been said as to the character of the " next war," and in view of considerations which will appear later, such an assumption needs to be scrutinized far more closely than is usually done. But for the moment we may let that pass; for undoubtedly part of the problem of war is the sense of being shut up to a choice of evils, so that though the way of battle is not an ideal exit from the dilemma, yet it often seems to the individual Christian the only honorable alternative to craven acquiescence in blatant wrong.

The problem of war for the Christian is frequently complicated by thinking of an army and navy in terms of a police force. One hears the plea advanced, for instance, by sincere lovers of peace that the British and American navies could between them police the high seas and so maintain the peace of the world against all comers! Or the role of international policeman is assigned to the League of Nations, and the threat of war by the league against any nation risking an appeal to arms is held out as a sufficient security against any such adventure.

Such hopes however are apt to be illusory; for the history of world politics goes to show that in the long run any endeavor to secure international peace by force or threat of coercion merely precipitates the very war it seeks to avoid.[2]

[2] This does not rule out the idea of an international police force, if the analogy of a civil police force be scrupulously observed; for the essence and efficiency of police action lies in the fact that it is the executor of public opinion against the lawbreaker: furthermore, the police operate in

The net result of " peace by force " is to encourage
preparations and combinations among the threatened
peoples until at last they feel themselves strong enough
in a military sense to challenge the self-appointed " po-
licemen " who undertake to preserve international harmony by *force majeure*. The situation is not unlike
that of *Punch's* irate parent on a public holiday, who
caught the ear of his tired and whimpering offspring
and demanded angrily, " Now then, are you going to
enjoy yourself or shall I make you ? " Human nature is
not made that way, and all attempts to impose peace
upon unwilling peoples break upon that stubborn fact.

Nevertheless, confusion between the soldier and the
policeman often forms a specious apologetic for the
maintenance of armaments, and no case against war
is adequate which ignores it. There are, of course, certain obvious and superficial differences between military and police action which strike any intelligent observer. For instance, the function of an army is to fight
the armies of other powers, but no one ever heard of
police forces being marshaled one against another in
order to give battle: consequently the efficiency or mag-
nitude of the police force in one city does not stimulate

a community where the civilians are unarmed and therefore incapable of
that organized warlike " aggression " which an army would be called upon
to resist. If these conditions were fulfilled in the international sphere, the
function of a league police force would not involve those military measures
which are usually contemplated when people speak of armed sanctions.
The question of an international police force is considered in detail in
Part 2 of this book, where the experience of police action under the
American federal system is presented as a parallel to a force under league
auspices.

other cities to competition in defense measures. But in the international world, the building of a battleship by one nation is invariably a challenge to other nations to do likewise; and so there inevitably emerges that competition in armaments which is one of the factors in the perpetuation of war. For, as Israel Zangwill truly puts it in his play *The War God:*

> . . . this wealth of ships and guns inflames the vulgar
> And makes the very war it guards against.

Again, the police deal directly with the lawbreaker or wrongdoer, and always without deliberate or intentional injury to the innocent citizen who may be at hand. It is, however, and always has been, one of the ironies of war that the chief culprits escape the retribution which poetic justice would bring upon them, and instead they become in many cases the heroes of their people and the belauded figures in national history. When an army fights, its shells and bullets and poison gas fall indiscriminately upon good and bad, innocent and guilty alike: the soldier deals with the enemy *en masse,* the policeman deals with him individually. So also, the police in endeavoring to restrain or apprehend the wrongdoer are merely the agents of an impartial judicial authority, and are themselves amenable to that authority, should they, in the discharge of their duty, violate any of the laws under which they act. An army, on the other hand, works under no recognized code of laws: or, more correctly, the law it observes is self-made and designed to suit its own requirements. The aim of military force is not to bring the enemy before an impartial court of justice, but by and of itself it acts as prosecution, judge, jury, jailer, and executioner in one; while in the process it seeks to inflict upon the enemy people the maximum of injury, harm, and destruction, alike to property and life.

It is to be observed in this connection that the forcible sanctions with which the League of Nations is endowed (see especially Article 16 of the Covenant, where the Council of the League is empowered to call for quotas of armed force from the constituent members of the league in case of necessity) approximate to a police function, in that the sanctions are never to be applied except under the authority and by the direction of the Council of the League. It is good to be able to recognize this as a step in advance upon the hitherto prevailing practice of competing and self-sufficient sovereignties acting through national armies; but it ought not to be confused with the true role of a police force, which differs from that of an army not only in the incidental and superficial difference already indicated, but also in certain things which are deeper and more fundamental.

These fundamental differences emerge when we judge both the military and the police systems by their ideals. If the ideal be good, then the system — though it be inadequate at present — can be progressively amended in the direction of the ideal; but if the ideal be itself intrinsically hurtful to human welfare, then any amendment or improvement of the system merely increases its capacity for ill. So then as between the police ideal and the military ideal. Ideally, the police system exists not to revenge itself upon an offender, and not merely to protect society from the depredations of a wrongdoer, but so to deal with the offender that he may be returned to society as a desirable citizen. It is true that this ideal is often obscured in practice, and that when it is a conscious aim it is often expressed in an ineffective way; but the ideal is there, and it is possible for any police system to develop in that direction. Such an ideal, however, only needs to be stated in order to reveal its complete opposition to the ideal under which an army is organized and acts; for the aim of an army is not to reform the offender, but to smash him; not to return the offender to his place and position in the world, but — as the Treaty of Versailles shows — to cripple his power and to rob him so far as is possible of the opportunity to recover. The antithesis indeed between the two ideals can be put in a single contrast when it is stated that the police ideal is redemptive and the military ideal destructive. This contrast is seen most acutely when we consider the actual methods by which a police force or an army operates; for the police exist in order to protect life and property, while an army functions by the destruction of life and property: or, in other terms, the power of the police is one of the prime buttresses of a law-abiding people, while the existence of armaments threatens the very civilization which has produced them.

The problem of war, therefore, in its impact upon the Christian conscience, is not to be disposed of by resolving it into terms of police tactics. The problem stands out starkly amid all the qualifications and sophistries with which it has been surrounded and by which at times the issue has been beclouded, because there is in the modern world and among thinking people a new realization of what war is in its fundamental processes and in its ultimate reactions; and at the same time there is a new and deeper understanding of the Person of Jesus Christ and his significance for the twentieth century. Can the processes of war and the gospel of Jesus ever be reconciled? and if not, what is the Christian's alternative to war? That is the problem before us.

CHAPTER II

THE AUTHORITY OF CHRIST

THE question of the legitimacy of war for the Christian rests in the last analysis upon an appeal to the authority of Christ; but it is necessary to realize where that authority is to be found and in what it consists. To many people that authority seems to have been dethroned by the processes and results of modern scholarship as applied to the Scriptures of the Old and New Testaments; time was when it was deemed sufficient to justify one's faith or conduct by citing an appropriate text; but " the devil can quote Scripture to his purpose," and the weakness of this method lies in the fact that the predilection of the person who quotes can easily be mistaken for the guidance of the Spirit. The writer visited one of the big penitentiaries in the Middle West of the United States recently, and the warder who acted as guide pointed with obvious pride to the electric chair in what is appropriately known as the " death chamber ": there was displayed the whole of the hideous paraphernalia associated with the scientific execution of the criminal, while around the walls were framed portraits and the fingerprints of some eighty odd men and women who had paid the extreme penalty of the law. Conversation inevitably drifted to the question of capital punishment, and the mere possibility of its ultimate abolition was received with indignant scorn by the warder: " Why," he said, " it's against nature, and what's more it's against religion! " This was interesting, and so he explained: " Don't the good Book say that when God was angry with men he destroyed them by water and then by fire? What's the difference if we destroy them by electricity? No, sir, capital punishment's a Christian institution! " The strict logician might murmur *non sequitur,* but neither Latin nor logic could refute Holy Writ, and there the matter ended!

The difficulty with the proof-text method, however, is that it entangles its devotees in inextricable moral dilemmas; thus, on the strict and literal authority of the Bible, they must be at one and the same time advocates and opponents of capital punishment, they must be both slaves and free men, polygamists and monogamists, warriors and pacifists; for it passes the wit of man to read an imprecatory Psalm as though it were the Sermon on the Mount, or to combine Joshua's treatment of his enemies with the reaction of Jesus toward his. The same difficulty arises if we confine our citations to the recorded words of Jesus himself: the opponent of war may quote the text, " resist not him that is evil," or insist upon Jesus' injunction to " love your enemies "; but during the World War eminent preachers and churchmen of all creeds found relief of conscience in such texts as, " I came not to bring peace but a sword," or " He that hath no sword, let him sell his

cloak and buy one "; or " Render to Cæsar the things
that are Cæsar's."   Sometimes indeed the proof-text
apologist struck a pitfall, as when the military representative on the statutory tribunal at Oxford sought to
dispose of the Quaker objection to war by the question:
" Did not Jesus say, ' An eye for an eye, and a tooth for
a tooth '? "   The so-called apocalyptic passages in the
Gospels and the forecasts of the violent doom of the
wicked in several of the parables of Jesus were also
prominent as phases of a Christian apologetic for a
" holy war."   Such instances could be multiplied many
times over both in condemnation of Christian participation in war and in favor of it; but it is obvious that
the issue can never be decided by rival quotations even
from the lips of Jesus himself.

In default of such decision, the authority of Christ
is sometimes sought by imagining the reaction of Jesus
if he were found in the context of the modern world.
The late Mr. W. T. Stead once published a Christmas
brochure under the title *If Christ Came to Chicago;* and
the best seller both in England and in America toward
the end of the nineteenth century was a naïve and sincere appeal to Christian people, written by an American minister, Dr. Charles M. Sheldon, and entitled *In
His Steps; or, What Would Jesus Do?* Any publication which thus focuses attention however crudely upon
the Person of Jesus Christ is bound to have a healthy
influence in the realm of morals; but the appeal of such
literature is as much to the imagination of the reader as
to the authority of Christ, for it is not easy to see Jesus

actually in the midst of life as we know it, and he was too profound and too startling a personality to enable anyone to predict with certainty where he would be found or how he would express himself in any modern situation with which we are familiar. In the early days of the World War, a well-known London preacher — whose spiritual insight was only equaled by his Christian courage — addressed a meeting in Manchester in the interests of peace: war-time passion had not then attained its full flood and he was accorded a courteous hearing by a large audience. At the close of his address a keen and convinced supporter of the then government, who was also a devout Christian, put the question: " Will Dr. —— say what he thinks Jesus would have done if he had been at the foreign office in August 1914? " And the reply was immediately forthcoming: " I can't imagine Jesus at the foreign office: can you? " It was an apt and clever answer, but it failed to convince just because the imaginations of questioner and speaker did not coincide: the court of appeal in both question and answer was the authority of Christ, but the personal equation of each man and his personal estimate of Christ's reaction to a given situation made it possible for authority to point in two directions at once. For the same reason, questions which were often put by both pacifist and bellicist (to use Sir Norman Angell's ugly but convenient word) failed to carry conviction or to make for agreement, so long as the questions required a common imagination for a common answer. Such questions were these: " Can you imagine Jesus

thrusting a bayonet into the body of his enemy?"
"Would Jesus don khaki?" "Would he approve the
slow starvation of innocent people by a blockade?"
These and similar questions were put by the pacifist,
and on the other side, these: "Do you think Jesus
would stand by with folded arms while Belgium was
being overrun?" "Would Jesus refuse to fight in order to save his native land from rapine and atrocity
and frightfulness?" In either case, it was the familiar,
inconclusive, unconvincing question, "What would
Jesus do?"

We must therefore find the authority of Christ in
something other than proof texts or our own estimate
of how he would act in a modern context. Even if we
could decide the latter question, we should not necessarily be nearer an authoritative solution of our ethical
difficulties; for one man's duty is not another's: differences of circumstance, capacity, opportunity, and above
all, differences of vocation make duty a matter which
cannot be prescribed *en bloc* for a multitude, but always something to which the individual is impelled by
his own conscience and which none can determine but
himself. Indeed, just here is to be found a fundamental defect of the usual military demand that it is every
citizen's duty to defend his country, the implication
always being that defense can only be conducted by
force of arms: apart altogether from the question of the
legitimacy of war from a Christian standpoint, the assumption that the moral duty of the citizen can be
scheduled by the state as a uniform task for all sorts

and conditions of men is something which strikes at the very roots both of human liberty and human responsibility. That the duty of great masses of men will be identical in a given emergency is not questioned, nor is it denied that duty may be suggested and encouraged along certain lines where common action is necessary for a common end: there are always those whose only duty in a bewildering situation is to submit to the direction of others who believe they have a clear vision of the needs of the moment. Such a situation arises when a nation is plunged into war; but if the warring state rides rough-shod over the convictions of conscientious citizens and seeks to coerce them into the regimented task of military service, it is inducing such men to be false to the duty which they feel to be laid upon them, and is in effect declaring that conscience is something which can be ignored at the demand of public expediency. To hold conscience in contempt, however, in an emergency is to teach men that it is of secondary account in all the affairs of life; for if it does not count in time of war, why should it count in time of peace? The last state therefore of a community which teaches such a lesson is apt to be worse than the first; for it is these incalculable moral assets which alone make a nation worth preserving; and consequently the statesman who invades the prerogatives of conscience in the name of "national duty" is doing an ill service to his country, and is always sacrificing the greater for the sake of the less. Here, of course, is the fatal objection to all systems of military conscription: for even if they be qualified by an adequate conscience clause[1] they assume that duty is a thing to be imposed from without instead of being accepted from within. The same assumption lay behind the retort of a friend when the present writer publicly pleaded on Christian grounds that conscription should not override conscience: " Do you think," asked the friend, " that you know better than the Archbishop of Canterbury? " The Archbishop had blessed the Conscription Act: but it was the first and only time that the writer had heard the idea of infallibility applied to an English ecclesiastic, and it is to be noted that it was applied not — as with the Pope — to matters of dogma, but to a matter of duty. The very controversy, however, which arose at that time over that issue showed that even in time of war duty was not regarded as entirely outside the range of personal responsibility. This estimate of the nature of duty is now generally admitted in most realms other than the military. It used to be held, of course, that duty could be prescribed in matters of religious worship, and the ages of persecution, with their Acts of Uniformity and their roll of martyrs, bear witness to the same folly and the same futility which still afflict the minds of men in regard to military service. But in the one case

---

[1] The British Military Service Acts during the World War made legal provision for the exemption of conscientious objectors but only in a few instances was the exemption operative, on account of the war-time passions which governed the adjudicating tribunals: the insuperable difficulty of devising a test by which conscience could be distinguished from less worthy impulses led to grave illegalities, and proved the impossibility of combining conscription with a due regard for the duty of the individual citizen.

as in the other, duty is a question not of a man's relation to the state or the church or any other external power, but only of his relation to God and his fidelity to what — in the particular circumstances of his own life — he feels to be God's will for him. The classic statement of a sense of duty is in Luther's defiance of the regimen prescribed by the Pope: " It is neither safe nor honest to do aught against conscience: here stand I: I can do no other: God help me: Amen! "

All this has a direct bearing upon the authority of Christ; for if it is not something which defines our exact duty as Christians, and if it is compatible with the utmost liberty of conscience, in what does it consist? The answer lies on the surface of the gospel story. The first disciples did not approach Jesus in the first instance as an authority to whom they were bound to submit, nor did they think of him at the outset in terms of " divinity," which laid down an inescapable law: they came to him first of all as a Man among men, one with whom they companied on the hillsides of Galilee or in the cities by the lake shore: but it was not long before they discovered that he " taught them as one having authority, and not as the scribes." Jesus has frequently been classed with other religious leaders and teachers: his name is often placed midway in a list beginning with Confucius or Moses, and ending with Darwin or Karl Marx; in the list may be included Plato and Augustine, Mohammed, Francis of Assisi, Francis Bacon, Kant, Goethe, Emerson, and, indeed, any and every man or woman who has contributed in any measure to the world's enlightenment; but, as has been re-marked,[2] such a juxtaposition gives a jar to the Christian reader, not because it is an offense against orthodoxy, but because it is an offense against decency. That is to say, we feel that somehow Jesus does not belong to a list like that, nor in fact to any other list which can be devised: indeed, it argues a certain lack of discrimination to place him in any list at all; for though there are doubtless elements in common which equate him with others of the world's teachers, yet in one obvious respect Jesus was unique, and he towers above every other teacher who ever taught. The distinction has been expressed by saying that while other teachers taught what was, Jesus *was* what he taught: others uttered the truth, but Jesus *was* the truth: in him precept and practice, teaching and action, perfectly coincided: he embodied and did not merely enunciate the things he proclaimed — with the result that the best commentary upon his words is his life, and the best interpretation of his life is in his words. Consider, for instance, the central note in the Christian ethic which is indicated by the word "love": the precepts and commands in the Gospels concerning "love" find their parallel in one form or another, either partially or completely, in other of the world's teachings: among pre-Christian writings, Confucius, Moses, and Gautama the Buddha can all be cited; yet until Jesus came — and for that matter since his day by those who ignore him — "love" was often misinterpreted as a mild senti-

[2] Dr. Carnegie Simpson in *The Fact of Christ*.

mentality, a sort of indulgent kindness which was always easy and good-natured. But, while the injunction to "love one another" has been common to all the world's greatest moralists, it was only Jesus who gave it precision and definition by saying, "this is my commandment, that ye love one another *as I have loved you.*" From that moment the world, if it cared to turn to the gospel-portrait, has known what "love" is, and no longer can we confuse it with what is merely soft and easy: in the light of that historic embodiment of love, we know that it is a passion which seeks always to make men at one with the life of God, and it uses any and every means to secure that end, except means which are themselves a violation of the divine holiness; for it is not only true that the end, however exalted, can never justify the means, but unless means and end are in moral harmony the one inevitably stultifies the other. Consequently, we find that the dealings of Jesus with his fellow men were not stereotyped or uniform, except in the impulse which moved him in his endeavor to win men from their sins and bring them into harmony with that Life of God for which they were created: his methods indeed were as varied as the human nature with which he had to deal: his constant aim, the dominating passion of his life, was to get the wrongdoer right, turn the sinner into a saint, make man at-one with God, and only on that basis make him at-one with his fellows. So, with sinners of a gross and obvious kind — the victims of bodily passion or social convenience — Jesus was usually tender, forgiving, even indulgent; for he believed in their power to "make good" in response to his encouragement and advice. With the Pharisees, nothing but drastic self-revelation could avail for repentance and righteousness: they must see themselves as they really were in all their hateful hypocrisy; and so with them Jesus was stern, seemingly cruel, inexorable in his exposure of their inmost souls. For some he used no other means than the power of prayer: with others — like Nicodemus or the Syrophœnician woman — he used quiet, persuasive argument or gentle irony: with his disciples — disputing over petty points of prestige — he was infinitely patient, and sought both by precept and by example to lead them in the way of divine rectitude.

But the climax of Jesus' love for men is seen in the closing events of the gospel story. For there in Jerusalem he faced, in one burning focus, every evil which had assailed him from the outset of his ministry; yet, on the plane of earthly action, there was at the last no way of defeating that evil except by compromise or meeting evil with evil; it was this dilemma which lay behind though it does no more than partially explain the awful agony of Gethsemane; for there he had either to allow evil to triumph — to wreck his ministry, obliterate his life, crush his friends, scatter his disciples, bring death and disaster upon innocent folk who trusted him (and all this he foresaw and foretold in apocalyptic warnings) — or else he had to resist aggressive evil with its own weapons, thrust his enemies aside heedless of their spiritual welfare, and so become part-

ner in the very sin from which he sought to redeem
them. In that dilemma, therefore, he did the hardest
thing that man can do when the assault of evil is
pressed; for he merely stood still, faithful to the will
and love of God, and allowed evil to nail him to the
cross. Yet in that seemingly impotent reaction to evil,
the purpose of his love was achieved: for, however we
explain it (and that is the province of theology), the
vision of that Man upon the cross, hating the sin which
murdered him and yet praying for the very men who
sinned, somehow stirs the soul, as no punishment or
penalty could do, to repentance and recoil, and so to
oneness with the life of God. But the cross was not
the end, it was only a beginning; for the story of the
resurrection — whatever we make of it as literal history
— is a witness to the fact that the love of Jesus was not
obliterated even by death; for he returned to the very
world which had rejected him, not to bring judgment
or vengeance, but to be for evermore the Friend and
Savior of all who give to him the allegiance of mind
and heart and will.

Whenever we face this gospel story and seize the
significance of its unrivaled love, we touch the secret
of the authority of Christ. For the gospel-portrait,
taken in its entirety, requires not only intellectual judgment on our part, but also moral decision: that is to say,
we do not merely ask what manner of Man he was, but
the practical issue is thrust upon us: Are we, amid the
circumstances of our life, for Jesus or against him? Do
we endorse the spiritual values for which he stood, or

do we despise them? The questions may be ignored, but once faced they cannot be evaded, for they are enforced by a sense of obligation: in other words, we know that we *ought* to live as he lived, and that the spirit and attitude to life which were his ought to be ours, from the greatest to the smallest activity of our being. Here again Jesus differs from other world-teachers: there is much in those other lives which is admirable, but in other respects we would not be what they were even if we could: genius so often is another name for the eccentric, and consequently while we admire it from a distance, we have generally no desire to imitate it. Devotees of Thomas Carlyle, for instance, never wished to change shoes with his wife, and the letters of Jane Welsh Carlyle have justified their hesitation! It means that, despite all the inspiration which Carlyle brought to multitudes, he never laid his disciples under a sense of obligation to share his temper and outlook. But one of the remarkable things about Jesus was the fact that he seemed such a normal member of the human race: there was much in him that baffled the understanding even of his intimates, but there was no suggestion of eccentricity, and men and women everywhere had the sense not only that his life was eminently livable, but that they ought so to live. But this sense of obligation did not pass with the bodily presence of Jesus, nor was it the monopoly of his contemporaries: on the contrary, it has come to all who in every age have faced the fact of Christ with intellectual integrity and with moral honesty; and the same is true

today. Even when, as is often the case, Christianity is
dismissed by men of the world as impracticable, there
is the tacit, if not avowed, admission that the world
ought to be such as to allow Christian values to become operative. It is but another aspect of the sense of
obligation which derives from the Person of Jesus.

That, of course, is why, historically, new values have
attached to right and wrong since Jesus lived: a new
standard of moral judgment and a new sense of sin
came into the world with him, and things which men
had previously accepted without question began to be
suspect. Jesus Christ became a fact of conscience. It
is, for example, no accident that one after another of
the world's time-honored iniquities have disappeared
from Christendom: the gladiator was the first to go:
the status of womanhood is always a test of the Christian standards implicit in any community, and it needs
but a casual comparison between a society influenced
by such standards and one from which they are absent
to see at once the reaction of Christianity in creating a
new conscience in regard to womanhood. In our own
day, dueling and chattel slavery have gone because
they were condemned by the Christian conscience; and
so one might go through a catalogue of earthly ills
which have been successively challenged and routed
because they were at variance with the way of life and
love which men see in Jesus Christ. But the Christian
conscience does not stand still: it is not static but dy-
namic, and other iniquities are therefore being challenged as our modern civilization is brought under the

scrutiny of a Christian judgment. One of the principal of these is war, and all the questions which gather about it: this, indeed, is likely to be the next great issue with which Christianity will have to deal; for, as has already been indicated, either civilization must be reorganized on a warless basis, or else it is doomed, and with it Christianity itself would be jeopardized. Not for the first time in history, practical expediency and a sense of Christian obligation are found to coincide.

This sense of obligation, however, implies something else which also bears upon the authority of Christ. Indeed, a sense that we are obliged to do a thing and a recognition of authority always go hand in hand. This conjunction is not confined to the realm of religion: religious authority is merely one example of a universal principle which applies as truly to the multiplication-table as to the ethics of Jesus; for when we admit that two and two make four we recognize in effect that mathematical truth is not something private and per-sonal to us — a matter of individual predilection — but is an expression of something which belongs to the very constitution of the universe: the truths of physical science are as valid in the furthest confines of space as they are in the humblest affairs of earth: the spectrum, which the physicist obtains with a blowpipe and a prism in a laboratory, enables the astronomer to an-nounce the chemical composition of the fixed stars. And so everywhere. It might be a convenience to rogues and thieves if two and two sometimes made five, but we know that in our practical everyday deal-

ings with one another we " ought " — we are under
an obligation which we cannot argue but which we are
bound to accept — to act on the principle that two and
two make four: to do otherwise is to be dishonored
before God and our own conscience. In other words,
the multiplication-table has authority because our sense
of obligation tells us that it is a part of the intrinsic
nature of things; or in religious phraseology, it is, on
the physical plane, an expression of the will of God.

The same applies to the authority of Christ. We read
the story of his life and seize the significance of his
Personality, and forthwith there is laid upon us a sense
of obligation which we may defy but which we cannot
dispute: for his words and witness carry an immediate
and instinctive conviction to all who consider them dis-
passionately with an open mind and a ready will. But
obligation here, as elsewhere, implies that the thing
we " ought " to do is a part of the moral order of the
universe: human judgments may differ as to how to
carry obligation into practice; but the standard we are
called to obey is as much an element in the essential nature of things as is the multiplication-table; or, again
to use religious phraseology, it has authority because it
bespeaks the presence of God. Yet it is to be noted that
we reach this conclusion not by arguing from a preconceived dogma as to Christ's " divinity," but solely
through the processes of our own experience as we confront the fact of Jesus Christ. His authority, therefore,
rests in the last analysis not on anything external, but
on the fundamental spiritual likeness between his na-

ture and ours: as we face the picture of that Man living and dying in a human context 1900 years ago, " deep calleth unto deep," and the conviction smites home to our hearts that in him we see what has been called " the human life of God himself." [3]   We thus affirm the fundamental dogma of our Christian faith; for we discover that Jesus was the embodiment or incarnation of the essential spirit and character of God; and it is for this reason that our God-given human nature agrees with and responds to the godlike in him.   In that fact and in no other is to be found the authority of Christ; and in the light of that fact we can say that the Christian way is the only way which can claim the endorsement of Almighty God or possibly win in a God-governed world.   In all the concerns of life, therefore, we are called to yield our soul's obedience to his authority.

[3] Henry van Dyke in *The Gospel for an Age of Doubt.*

CHAPTER III

THE NATURE OF WAR: ON THE BATTLE FRONT

If we are to bring the institution of war to the test of Christ's authority — and no other test has final validity for the Christian man or woman — we must first of all strip war of the illusions which surround it and see it as it really is in its essential nature. No one will question the heroism of the battlefield, yet this alone is not enough to give the processes of war a Christian character or to make them compatible with the will of God in Jesus Christ.

It is essential therefore at the outset not to be misled by terms that are loosely applied. For instance, the glory and splendor of death for the sake of one's country has been, and still is, a familiar appeal in the justification of war; and the fact that the cross of Christ is centered in the sacrifice of death is frequently taken as establishing an equation between Calvary and the battlefield. During the World War one of the most familiar cartoons issued for the consolation of Christian parents, suddenly bereaved by the death of their sons in action, depicted Jesus, with the marks of his wounds still visible, bending over the dying warrior and bestowing his blessing. No word should be uttered which in any wise seems to depreciate the element of sacrifice in the soldier's deed; for no man can engage in war without the knowledge that for him it may involve the surrender of life or limb, the loss of sight or reason, the permanent impairing of health, and must in any case involve intense and agonizing strain upon nerve and physique, even if it does not actually issue in wounds and bodily suffering. All this the soldier faces in a spirit of true sacrifice, and it is this which ennobles his calling and gives to it a certain religious value. But to think of war thus in terms of self-sacrifice is at best only a half-truth; for we befool ourselves when we represent the essence of war as a willingness to die or to sacrifice oneself. Before all else, war involves on the part of the soldier a readiness to kill and to sacrifice not self but others; and only as we face that fact do we rightly assess its moral quality. If war were waged solely on the principle of *self*-sacrifice, there might be martyrdom, but there could be no battle.

The civilian apologist for war is generally loath to contemplate this element of killing; but at least the military man is under no such illusion. In a debate on military punishment in the House of Commons on April 12th, 1932, a military member, supporting the retention of the death penalty on active service, stated his own experience in these words: " War was an extremely bloody business, and they must remember that when all was said and done it was a soldier's job to kill! " When the United States of America entered the war in 1917, and the first American troops landed in England, a service of dedication was held in St. Paul's

Cathedral. The Stars and Stripes were unfurled, and
Julia Ward Howe's "Battle Hymn of the Republic"
was sung:

> As He died to make men holy,
> Let us die to make men free.

But if that vast congregation had been asked to sing
(what indeed was the actual truth) "Let us *kill* to
make men free," the whole concourse would have been
shocked and horrified. Yet, robbed of its glamour, that
is what war is! Even in time of war, however, the
comfortable illusion was cultivated by the civilian
population that killing was a quite secondary and subordinate element in battle, and press and people alike
spoke habitually as though war, so far at least as their
own soldiers were concerned, was always and entirely
a display of *self*-sacrifice.

But there are also other elements in war besides the
act of organized killing, which need to be taken into
account if we would properly assess its moral quality
and escape the illusions which surround the subject.
Something will be said in the following chapter of the
nature of war on what has been called "the home
front" — its reaction upon the common contacts of
civilian life and its contempt for all the elementary
moralities of human relationship. But here we confine
our analysis to the battle front.

Mr. Winston Churchill is our authority for the statement that in the World War "every outrage against
humanity or international law was repaid by reprisals

often on a greater scale and of longer duration." [1]
Those are short memories which do not recollect how
the first air-raids over London were greeted with
horror-stricken condemnation by the British public:
the German airmen were denounced as " baby-killers "
who made war on women and children, and the whole
proceedings were stigmatized as at once un-British and
un-Christian. Yet within a month the honorable protest of the Archbishop of Canterbury had been silenced,
and reprisals upon the Rhineland cities were part of
the regular British (and presumably Christian!) retort
to the attacks upon London. The German Chancellor
was held up to the scorn of the civilized world when
in 1914 he justified the invasion of Belgium on the
ground of "military necessity," but as the war proceeded it became clear that this same necessity governed each and all of the belligerents; for in war every
consideration is perforce subordinate to the attainment
of victory: no scruples must be allowed to intervene;
and when once the determination of an issue is made
to depend upon violence, the overpowering of the
enemy becomes the dominating objective. Hence the
moral, social and physical well-being of men counts as
nothing if it conflicts with this objective: as any army
manual indicates, moral considerations are not only
irrelevant, they are an intrusion when military requirements are at stake. That is to say, an army is impossible unless the soldier in certain particulars surrenders
his moral judgment, his conscience, his will, to the dis-

[1] *The World Crisis,* by Winston Churchill.

cretion of his military superior; for it has to be remembered that the soldier — at least in the less exalted ranks — is denied the option of resignation which belongs everywhere to civil life when conscience and the command of a superior conflict. In war, law — whether moral or statute — ceases to count, the Sermon on the Mount is an impertinence, the end justifies the means, and the well-being of neither friend nor foe weighs as against victory. In civil life, any man who acted according to the so-called " ethics of war " would be outlawed from decent society, and, even if he did not speedily find himself behind prison bars, he would be regarded universally as (in Theodore Roosevelt's phrase) an " undesirable citizen." But such is the moral perversion of war that the very vices of civil life become the virtues of military life.

This fact becomes tragically apparent if we take note of the way in which the ordinary decencies of human intercourse are treated in war. Take chivalry, for instance. For centuries the illusion has been cherished that the man under arms is the embodiment of all that is chivalrous toward both friend and foe: in the traditional stories of armored knighthood he appears as the defender of womanhood, the rescuer of fair ladies, the champion of the helpless; and to these same noble qualities war still makes its appeal; for in every war the cry is raised, " women and children in danger." But when in response to this appeal the recruit has been trained, what does he find? Where, for example, is chivalry toward one's foes to be found in this piece of advice, taken from a military manual for use in the United States Army? "Bayonet fighting is possible only because red-blooded men naturally possess the fighting instinct. This inherent desire to fight and kill must be carefully watched for and encouraged by the instructor. To finish an opponent who hangs on, or attempts to pull you to the ground, always try to break his hold by driving the knee or foot to his crotch and gouging his eyes with your thumbs. Men still have fight in them unless you hit a vital spot. But when the bayonet comes out and the air sucks in and they begin to bleed on the inside, they feel the pain and lose their fight." [2]

If anyone wishes to know something of the way in which war cancels out chivalry toward women, he can do no better than read the history of the Contagious Diseases Acts, or of the long heroic struggle of Josephine Butler to secure the abolition of *maisons tolereés* in British Army quarters. To suggest that war either defends or respects womanhood is one of those persistent lies by which a foul and hideous immorality is made to appear respectable. Chivalry in its true and Christian sense never has been, and never can be, associated with a process which segregates vast bodies of men from their own womankind and encourages the beast in human nature to run loose; and it is significant that in time of war licensed prostitution and other

[2] Quoted in *The World To-morrow*, New York, February 1926. In response to protests by sensitive people who dislike to face facts, the paragraph has been modified in later editions of the Manual, but this classic remains as a revelation of war's chivalry in dealing with an opponent.

sexual abominations associated with the Contagious Diseases Acts invariably reappear under official sanction and control. The public at home is not told these things while a war is in progress, and it is not pleasant to speak of them when a war is over; but if we are rightly to assess the moral quality of war the unsavory facts of army immorality have to be taken into account as one of the things which make war what it is. Signor Nitti, ex-Premier of Italy, has said: " The losses in human life and property, great as they are, are small evils compared to the undermining of morals and the lowering of standards of culture and civilization." [3] Mr. Sherwood Eddy tells how he held evangelistic meetings during the war in camps and hospitals. " In one place," he says, " the commanding officer informed me that over 80,000 men had been down with venereal disease in that one hospital alone." [4] Prophylaxis against venereal disease was part of the regular provision of some of the armies on active service; and, according to an eye-witness who refers to the long strain of the war on the troops, " the authorities began to give frequent leave and to encourage the boys either openly or tacitly to ' find a woman ' and get thoroughly satisfactorily drunk." [5] At the close of the World War Sir Philip Gibbs wrote a book under the title, *Now It Can be Told;* but the standing difficulty about the na-

[3] *The Decadence of Europe,* by Nitti.

[4] *The Case Against War,* by Sherwood Eddy.

[5] *The Next War,* by Will Irwin. This refers, of course, only to that portion of the front under the witness's observation, and it would be unfair to regard it as a generalization.

ture of war is that not one-tenth of its revolting bestiali-
ties and immoralities can ever be told; for, fortunately
or otherwise, language is too weak and ineffective a
medium to describe a process at once so complex, so
mean and filthy and cowardly, so stark and ugly in its
moral aspect, and yet in certain other of its aspects so
splendid and heroic.

When, however, we bring war to the test of the authority of Christ, it is not *one* of its aspects, but the thing
as it is in its *every* aspect which must be subject to our
scrutiny. When Christian people justify the way of the
battlefield, they justify courage and loyalty and devotion and self-sacrifice; but they also endorse destruction
and violence and meanness and immorality, and every
item in the gamut of human vice; and the problem has
to be faced as to whether or not this can be done in the
name of Jesus Christ and with the sanction of our
Christian faith.

But war in the modern world is a process in which the
civilian as well as the soldier has a part, and the " home
front," therefore, must be considered before we turn to
the relation between war and Christianity.

CHAPTER IV

THE NATURE OF WAR: ON THE HOME FRONT

THE waging of war in days not very far behind us used to be a matter of comparatively small professional armies directed by governments which — even when functioning under the forms of democracy — were in practice oligarchical and not too intimately dependent upon the peoples they governed. Shortly after the World War we learned with astonishment, almost with incredulity, and with a certain degree of amusement, that a trapper in the Canadian Yukon was unaware of the events which were shaking the world until late in 1918 he hit the trail for Dawson City, and there heard that a four-years' conflict had taken place, and that the victorious Allies were drafting terms of peace. But in days gone by, in the remoter parts of all the countries of Europe, this must have been a common experience with great sections of the community. Even during the Napoleonic Wars, when all Europe was aflame, Goethe went on with his literary work, undisturbed in body and in mind, though actually living within a few miles of the Franco-German frontier: the waging of war was to him merely a minor disturbance amid the absorbing problems of human life. So too, in the same period, there is singularly little awareness of war's alarms in the records of the Evangelical Revival which was then sweeping through England, and men were free to devote their thought and energy to the things of the Spirit, undeterred by those political and military upheavals which dominate the history of that age. Even when the populace was aware of such things, the interest was sporadic; for wars were protracted over ten, fifteen or twenty years, and the critical battles which determined the fate of empires and changed the map of the world were infrequent and comparatively small affairs. There is significance in the fact, for instance, that only about 20,000 British troops took part in the Battle of Waterloo, and far less than that number in the remoter conflicts of Crecy and Agincourt. War was then merely one department of state activity, and was the concern of the statesman rather than of the people as a whole. Even as late in British history as the Boer War, at the end of the nineteenth century, the conflict after the first few months failed to dominate public interest, and, as the newspapers of that date indicate, the ordinary activities of trade and sport and politics retained their place as the leading concerns of the day.

But nowadays all that has changed. The application of scientific invention has made modern war no longer a matter of strategic maneuvering punctuated by occasional battles, but a sustained and intensive conflict under conditions of permanent entrenchment, and from which there is no release day or night, in season or out of season. Where in bygone days cities were beleaguered,

now whole nations are reduced by blockade and starvation: moreover, the advent of aircraft has carried the
actual clash of battle far beyond the zone of the contending armies, and the civilian population is brought within
the orbit of bombardment and destruction formerly confined to the military forces. A "next war," should it
occur, will intensify and still further widen the area of
such operations; for enemy aircraft on both sides would
have as their objective the sudden and speedy oblitera-
tion of the home bases by which the armies are maintained, and the infliction of defeat by destroying both
the civilization and the morale of the opposing nation
or nations. The fact that, as has been indicated, the
process would be mutual and that both sets of combatants would go down in a common ruin, only gives
added point to the truth that modern war is waged not
only on a battle front, but quite as much — or indeed
even more so — on what is known as the home front.

This fact has an important bearing upon the nature
of war, especially in its moral aspect; and it is something
which ought not to be omitted from consideration when
we test the processes of war by the authority of Christ.
For since modern war touches the whole populace, it is
necessary for the warmaker today to enlist the assent
and consent of the citizenry generally, not only to the
initial declaration of war, but still more to the prosecution of war, despite the suffering and disaster which fall
upon the civilian population as an inevitable price of an
appeal to arms. In the familiar jargon which became
current during the World War, the " morale of the

people " must be maintained at all costs; and it is in pursuing this end that modern war reveals some of its ugliest features. Yet, if war is to be endorsed and supported, these features must be included among the things we approve; for ultimately means and end are one, and he, therefore, who wills the end which the act of war seeks to secure also wills the dreadful means by which war is carried — as the ironic phrase has it — to " a successful conclusion."

Chief among the activities of the home front in time of war is the deliberate debauching of the public mind by means of both official and unofficial propaganda. In various ways mob psychology is exploited; for — as the stories both of the Russian Revolution in 1917 and of the final German collapse in 1918 demonstrate — a modern war stops the moment that popular passion cools below fever heat. This is so well understood both by the military and the civil authorities that immediate steps are taken to prevent — or to stifle if it arises — any kind of *rapprochement* or fraternization either between the warring peoples or between the troops on the opposing sides. It is a crime punishable by fine and imprisonment to write a letter, even of the most innocuous kind, to a friend belonging to a nation with which one's own nation is at war. Direct postal facilities, of course, cease to exist, but even communication through neutrals is forbidden: for this purpose a strict censorship is instituted, and private correspondence for places beyond the frontier is scrutinized and mutilated by an army of elderly clerks who are too old or too infirm to fight. It is called " doing one's bit," and the fact that it is a task subversive of the accepted decencies of human intercourse does not make it any the less respectable or even laudable in time of war. The late Mr. E. D. Morel, the outspoken critic of the Congo régime under King Leopold of Belgium, wrote in 1917 a letter to his friend, M. Romain Rolland, in Switzerland, and suggested the possibility of getting the interest of certain anti-militarist groups in Germany in securing an honorable peace by negotiation. Whether the actual suggestion was wise or practicable is not to the point: the nature of war on the home front is shown by the sequel; for, convicted of the crime of desiring a cessation of human slaughter, Mr. Morel was sentenced to six months' hard labor. The will to fight had to be maintained, no matter what happened to peace-loving citizens!

By such a statement no reflection is intended or implied upon the sincerity of the statesmen responsible for the conduct of any given war: by the very terms of their deepest convictions, a war must be fought to a finish; and a conflict, therefore, which threatens to stop half-way because enemies across the frontiers or on the field become friends is a betrayal of the very cause for which war is undertaken. There was one very significant illustration of this state of mind comparatively early in the progress of the World War. The press censorship had not become very rigid by the end of 1914, and it was still deemed not inconsistent with patriotism or with an effective prosecution of the war to allow accurate reports from the battle front to appear in print: consequently, it was known generally that on the first Christmas Day of the war an unofficial truce was called between the British and German troops on certain sections of the front: the trench parapets were lined with candles, and Christmas-trees were placed in position here and there along the line: " no-man's-land," between the lines, which was usually a grave-yard, became alive with groups in which khaki and field-grey were indiscriminately mixed: chocolate and the ubiquitous cigarette were freely exchanged for samples of German rations, and the soldiers discovered that the " enemy " consisted of men " of like passions with themselves." Such was the story carried by the press in England. But suddenly the news changed: the men were back in the trenches, periscopes took the place of candles, and rifles glinted where the Christmas-trees had stood. Something had happened to change friendliness back into enmity. Sir Ian Hamilton has told us what it was in his book, *The Friends of England*. " Under cover of the battle smoke," he says, " many of the rank and file had made an effort to hold out to one another bloodstained hands. Once even, the Anglo-Saxons and the Saxons had come to a tacit understanding that they would not kill each other on Christmas Day: so they actually mingled and sang hymns and songs. ' This shows a feeling which we must stamp out as if the house was catching fire,' said a certain high official at my table; and duly the feeling was stamped out! " Behind that final observation lay the deliberate transfer of the fraternizing troops to other sectors; for it was discovered that where men had mingled as fellow creatures and brothers, they could not be induced to obey the order to fire or to treat a " brother " as an " enemy." So " duly the feeling of comradeship was stamped out " in order that the fratricide of war might proceed! Rumor has it that the " high official " whom Sir Ian Hamilton quotes is now a well-known politician; but the point to be observed is that it was not the exigencies of battle but those of statecraft which required the ending of the Christmas truce. It was war on the home front, not on the battle front, which thus foreclosed the possibility of substituting a universal handshake for universal strife.

It has been said that " the first casualty in war is Truth," and certainly the history of wartime propaganda justifies that dictum; for no one can even dip into the record of carefully disseminated fictions and slanders and falsehoods without recognizing that the cynic did not exaggerate when he said that " propaganda is a longer way of spelling lie." Yet, so long as a war is in progress, even to question the accuracy of any statement discreditable to the enemy people is to incur the odium of being dubbed a traitor or worse. Canon Lyttelton had the courage in the autumn of 1914 to admit, when pressed for particulars, that a statement to which he had given currency as to the " crucifixion " of a Canadian soldier by the Germans was based merely upon hearsay, and immediately there arose the cry that such want of patriotism made him unfit to continue as headmaster of Eton. Cause and effect may not have been so closely associated as the public was led to believe, but it was not long before Canon Lyttelton had retired and Eton had another head! Lord Morley, in recalling his own attitude during a previous war, says: " Argument has little chance after war has once got under full way. As John Adams put it in 1776: ' a torrent is not to be impeded by reasoning, nor a storm by ridicule.' That is the worst of war; it ostracizes, demoralizes, brutalizes Reason: . . . hate takes root as a tradition, and lasts." [1] In other words, war on the home front is stimulated and maintained, not at the demand of a calm, dispassionate judgment applied to the issue before the nations, but at the behest of an unreasoning passion which is blind to every consideration except the achievement of victory.

It is the task of propaganda to maintain this passion at white heat, for without it the people will tire of the conflict and seize a too early opportunity of peace. The diatribes by politicians, press, and even preachers during the World War against what was called " war weariness " were an evidence of the nervousness of the leaders of public opinion lest the battle should be drawn before the enemy was defeated. Hence, every suggestion for the conclusion of hostilities — especially if the initiation of such suggestion could be traced to the other side — was contemptuously described as a " peace trick ": so too kaisers and kings and presidents and prime ministers, to say nothing of lesser political lights, in every country buoyed up the morale of their people by extravagant prospects of imminent victory, even though —

[1] Lord Morley, *Recollections,* vol. 2.

as post-war confessions have revealed [2] — they were well aware of the stubborn stalemate on the battle front. The fighting instinct and the determination to hang on at all costs were fed, as the war proceeded, by baser and ever baser appeals: a British statesman played up to the sporting instinct by using the vernacular of the ring, and exhorted his hearers to " fight to a finish," until they had administered a " knockout blow ": the Germans retorted by their " Hymn of Hate "; in order to stimulate the evil passions upon which war feeds, a medal was struck in Munich to celebrate the sinking of the Cunard liner, the " Lusitania," by a German submarine.[3] The humorous weeklies and the cartoonists of every country represented the enemy group of nations as vermin too loathsome to be treated with anything less than extinction; and the music, the literature, the art, indeed the entire civilization of the enemy was held up to contempt as something lower than the crudest savagery.

These things were partly effect and partly cause: they were the natural reaction of war upon the beast which is always latent in human nature, while on the other hand they were deliberately used and fostered by those in authority in order to cultivate the war-temper, and so make it possible for statesmen to realize the ideal of

[2] See, in particular, *The Intimate Papers of Colonel House*, Page's *Life and Letters*, Lord Grey of Fallodon's *Twenty-five Years*, Lloyd George's *War Memoirs*, and other volumes dealing with war-time politics.

[3] This, however, was not an official act, as alleged in England at the time, but a piece of private enterprise in the task of propaganda: see Ponsonby's *Falsehood in War Time* for particulars.

victory which they were convinced was necessary to their country's weal.[4] If the enemy, however, was represented as all-black, the Allies were all-white (or all whitewash in some cases!): they were invariably " our noble allies," fighting disinterestedly in the cause of liberty and culture and civilization, even though behind the scenes the statesmen of every country were signing secret treaties [5] agreeing to the partition of enemy empires on the principle of " the spoil to the victors." Thus, Russia was to have Constantinople (the Tsar, despite his Siberian brutalities, was then the " noble ally " of Britain and France), France and Britain were

---

[4] The demoralizing effect of war upon the civil population is seen in every age: an appeal to violence means the abdication of reason and all the common decencies of human intercourse on the part of those who endorse the appeal to arms. Consider, as a typical example, the lot of the " loyalists " during the American War of Independence. Professor George M. Wrong tells the story in his *History of Canada:* " It is likely that the sympathies of at least one-third of the colonists were with the British side. But . . . we hear of Loyalist clergymen dragged from their pulpits and maltreated; of Loyalists who were whipped through the streets and had their ears cropped; of other Loyalists covered with tar and then rolled in feathers taken from their own beds, or held astride of the sharp edge of a rail and made to take a rough ride which involved acute pain: or held under water and brought to the surface to breathe and then ducked again: or tied roughly to a post, with some dead animal dangling beside them. . . . Even the mild Washington said that the best thing that Loyalists could do was to commit suicide. John Adams, who became the second President of the United States, said that they ought to be hanged: Benjamin Franklin, the grave philosopher, had no pity on them. . . . Even after the war, the bitterness against them was frantic. In hell, wrote one versifier, the most evil spirits would turn in loathing from an Englishman: George III, to whom the Loyalists adhered, was a crowned ruffian, his statesmen were scoundrels, his sailors were pirates, and his people were degraded slaves."

[5] The text of those treaties is now published in a little volume by F. Seymour Cocks, entitled *The Secret Treaties.*

to carve up the Asiatic empire of Turkey; or, on the other side, Germany and Turkey were to swallow, if they could not digest, large slices of Russia. Such agreements, when from time to time the secrets leaked out, were justified as part of the price of holding a military alliance together, and the peoples for the most part were so intoxicated by " propaganda " that they still acknowledged the " nobility " of allies who thus needed to be bribed into loyalty or paid for their disinterested services! These facts are not recalled for the sake of reproach but in the interests of a true diagnosis of war. Admittedly, a statesman responsible for the conduct of a war is in a position where desperate expedients have to be adopted, even though they go against the grain; for when once victory is the supreme objective nothing can be allowed to stand in its way. But it is precisely this fact which gives to war on the home front its characteristic nature, and which therefore must be taken into account when we assess its moral quality or bring it under the judgment of Christ.

Yet it was not only in large issues of political policy that the demoralization of war was seen in the years 1914–18. The story of official propaganda during the World War is at times so mean and petty, and at the same time so vindictive, as to make it almost unbelievable that sane and normally honorable men and women could stoop to it. Again the motive is not questioned; but it is part of the essential nature of war that the finest motives must always be betrayed by the actual processes which are necessary to the prosecution of war: in war,

whether on the battle front or on the home front, the
best of men must always contradict by his methods the
very motive that impelled him to resort to war. So it
comes to be, not only that truth is sacrificed and evil
passion inflamed, but falsehoods are purposely invented
and circulated; the vocation of the spy, the eavesdropper,
the decoy, becomes an honorable calling: devices which
would be spurned with contempt in time of peace are
the accepted canons of respectable folk; and the whole
of civil life is honeycombed with suspicion and mutual
fear. The British War Office, and presumably all
others, freely used *agents provocateurs* in its endeavor to
entangle those who were deemed to be too critical of its
doings or not sufficiently ardent in support of a fight to
a finish. Mr. Ramsay MacDonald, at that time treasurer
of the Labor party, had to complain in the House of
Commons of the unwelcome attentions of such creatures; and the present writer was one of several whom
the authorities sought to trap into utterances or actions
which could be construed as " seditious." On one occasion two decoys, thinly disguised as clerics, endeavored to secure from him encouragement in dodging
the Military Service Acts, which would immediately
have been laid as evidence on a charge of violating the
Defense of the Realm Act. The attempt failed, however, for it is no part of a Christian peace witness to urge
others to act upon convictions which they do not hold;
and the essence of Christian liberty is freedom to go
wrong as well as right. To challenge another man's
conscience and call him to face the nature of war as a

Christian is one thing, to prescribe his duty in the light of someone else's conscience is another; and even in time of war there were English magistrates who recognized the distinction and, despite a good deal of public opprobrium, acted upon it.

The *agent provocateur,* however, had other tasks to perform than impersonation. He attended meetings, and even religious services, and took voluminous notes: and he raided houses, offices and public buildings, to discover letters, papers or books which might justify prosecution.

Ignorant men for the most part filled this unworthy role, and they not unnaturally showed little discrimination in the material they seized. The writer was cited as a witness in a case at Altrincham near Manchester in 1916, where the police agent had seized as seditious literature John Stuart Mill's *Essay on Liberty* and Bishop Gore's *Exposition of the Sermon on the Mount.* The New Testament was not included in the list, but the question of publishing biblical quotations was raised in the House of Commons, and Mr. J. M. Robertson replied on behalf of the government by saying: " If the Sermon on the Mount, or any other portion of any other sacred book, were used for the deliberate purpose of preventing men from enlisting or accepting enlistment, that would be a military offense." [6]   The implication is, of course, clear: " accepting enlistment " will not square with the Sermon on the Mount!   The following from the *Labor Leader,* January 14th, 1915, is significant:

[6] *Hansard,* June 29th, 1916.

"We submitted for publication without comment a number of quotations from the Bible, and these . . . were struck out by the censor."

The War Office knew, if the church did not, that war and the Sermon on the Mount could not coexist!

But that is to anticipate the theme of the next chapter. This chapter may be brought to a close with a few further illustrations of the nature of war, as typified by the propaganda of 1914–18.[7]

The manipulation of news, for instance, was one of the devices by which the war mood was maintained, and to this end anything which blackened the character of the enemy was good copy. Professor G. Lowes Dickinson has collected the following significant sequence of press reports,[8] which well illustrate the manner in which the peoples were at once fooled and embittered by journalists doing the bidding of their governments in the task of propaganda. In the *Cologne Zeitung,* in September 1914, it was reported that "when the fall of Antwerp was known the church bells were rung " (i.e. in Cologne). A few days later this appeared in the Paris *Matin* thus: "According to the *Cologne Zeitung,* the clergy of Antwerp were compelled to ring the church bells when the fortress was taken." The *London*

[7] The illustrations are confined to the activities of the Allies in the World War, not because similar things did not occur among the Central Powers, but because to an English writer the former are necessarily more accessible and familiar. For a well-documented and impartial examination of methods of propaganda in every belligerent country, see *Propaganda Technique in the World War,* by Professor Lasswell.

[8] *The Power of the Press for Peace and War,* published by the National Council for Prevention of War, Washington, D. C.

Times then copied and improved the report by saying: " According to what the *Matin* has heard from Cologne, the Belgian priests who refused to ring the church bells when Antwerp was taken have been driven from their places." Italy went one better, and the *Corriere della Sera* of Milan published this: " According to what the *Times* has heard from Cologne via Paris, the unfortunate Belgian priests who refused to ring the church bells when Antwerp was taken have been sentenced to hard labour." But it was left to the *Paris Matin* to add the supreme touch of imagination and falsehood by saying: " According to information to the *Corriere della Sera* from Cologne via London, it is confirmed that the barbaric conquerors of Antwerp punished the unfortunate Belgian priests for their heroic refusal to ring the church bells by hanging them as living clappers to the bells with their heads down."

In view of the above example of propaganda by legend, it is not surprising to learn that while Britain and France were full of tales of German " frightfulness," Germany was no less full of stories of Allied " atrocities." Nothing is to be gained by minimizing the appalling frightfulness of war, and German military theory undoubtedly intensified it as a deliberate policy: fortunately for the Allies, the opportunity of invasion never tempted them to similar extremes; but one had only to listen in England to the diabolical hate of all things German to recognize that if the opportunity was lacking the will was there: it was a commonplace to hear ordinarily good and humane men and women, incited by atrocity stories, urge a policy of measure for measure, or " do as we are done by," only more so. No one can possibly assess the infinite moral damage done by the orgy of hate and ill will, without which no war can be carried through. This is not incidental to war on the home front, it is essential to it, and is of its intrinsic nature: human flesh and blood, to say nothing of the human soul, would weary of the whole ghastly business, were it not for the carefully calculated infusion of evil passion by the official propaganda departments of every government involved.

Some frank confessions of this fact have been made by men " in the know," since the close of the World War. Admiral Sims, for instance, who was United States Naval Commander during the war, said in an interview: [9] " One of the sacrifices that people must necessarily make during wartime is of an accurate knowledge of events. You have got to keep many facts from your own people to keep them from the enemy. It would be extremely unpatriotic for a newspaper to tell the absolute truth about what is taking place during a war, even if the newspaper could get the absolute truth." [10]

[9] *New York Tribune*, June 1923.

[10] Admiral Sims in the same interview went on to give a few enlightening particulars: he stated, for instance, that " there was no authentic record of an atrocity ever having been perpetrated by the commander and crew of a German submarine, and the press accounts of the terrible atrocities were nothing but propaganda." When challenged by correspondents nurtured on wartime fables, the Admiral stuck to his point by declaring: " I stated that, barring the case of the hospital ship, ' Llandovery Castle,' I did not know of any case where a German submarine commander had fired upon the boats of a torpedoed vessel, and that the submarine commanders generally acted in a humane manner."

The sinking of the "Lusitania" by a German submarine came as a shock in 1915 even to people already inured to daily reports of wartime horrors, but propaganda saw to it that the deed should seem even darker than it was; for it was persistently asserted in the British press that the vessel was a harmless merchantman, with nothing aboard that was contraband according to the so-called laws of war. Yet on May 9th, 1915, the *New York Times*[11] printed a statement by Mr. Herman Winter, assistant manager of the Cunard Line, that the "Lusitania" on her fatal voyage carried 4,200 cases of cartridges! The truth, however, was not allowed to appear in England.

In 1922, at a public dinner in New York,[12] a gentleman who was one of the correspondents of the *London Daily Mail* in Belgium during the German advance of August 1914, confessed with glee how he had invented the widely circulated story of the Belgian child whose hands were cut off after its father and mother had been killed. So much pity and indignation were excited by the story that offers poured into the *Daily Mail* office for the adoption of the child: the editor wired the correspondent to bring the child to England, and he promptly laid the child low with an attack of typhoid. Finally Queen Alexandra offered to provide for the child, and as things were becoming embarrassing for the correspondent, he wired that the victim

[11] America, of course, was not then in the war.
[12] Reported in the *New York Times* and quoted in the *London Crusader*, February 24th, 1922.

of atrocity had succumbed to shock and fever! But the
lie which the correspondent circulated appeared as part
of the Bryce Report on German atrocities, and it had a
long and evil life, and left behind it a trail of blood and
hate before it succumbed under the blaze of the unexpected truth!

A particularly brazen case of propagandist falsehood,
with enormous consequences of loathing and ill will,
was the statement, accompanied by photographs, that
the Germans were in the habit of sending their dead to
a " cadaver factory," where corpses were turned into
the commercial fat of which Germany was then in sore
need. The *New York Times* and other papers have told
how the story was invented and the photographs added.
A British general was its author: the general was associated with the " intelligence department," and there
came into his hands two pictures, one showing the
removal of dead horses to the " cadaver factory," and
the other showing the removal of dead soldiers for
burial. The rest was easy: he changed the titles, and
then forged a German diary and placed this in the
pocket of a dead German, where his men found it.[18]

A catalogue of war lies masquerading under the name
of propaganda would make an interesting study in
human gullibility; but Sir Philip Gibbs, the well-known
war correspondent, has anticipated the inevitable verdict upon such a catalogue when he says: " Greedy was
the appetite of the mob for atrocity tales, and the more

[18] Quoted by H. C. Engelbrecht, article on "How War Propaganda
Won," in *The World Tomorrow*, New York, April 1927.

revolting they were the quicker they were swallowed ";
and then he gives it as his judgment that " hatred at
home " was " largely inspired by feminine hysteria and
official propaganda." [14]

Such, then, are a few — a very few — illustrations of
war on the home front. Its weapons are not physical,
but psychological: a lie is often more potent for victory
than a bullet; and since hate and evil thinking among
the civil population are essential to the determination
which will " fight to a finish," these things must be encouraged and stimulated as a normal process of war and
in the name of " military necessity." Without them no
modern war could be sustained, and no people could
be induced to persist either in inflicting or enduring the
senseless slaughter of battle. It is thus of the very
nature of war that it not only kills the bodies of men,
but it also degrades and destroys all that is finest in
the soul.

[14] *Now It Can be Told*, by Philip Gibbs.

CHAPTER V

CHRISTIANITY AND WAR

In a sermon at Geneva during the sessions of the Assembly of the League of Nations, the preacher,[1] who had
himself approved the struggle of 1914–18, but had later
seen the nature of war both on the home and the battle
fronts, declared that " War is the world's greatest collective sin "; and in view of the foregoing analysis of the
processes of war, few if any Christian people will dissent
from his judgment. The authority of Christ and the
nature of war are in sharp and irreconcilable opposition.

We shall not do fairly, however, by those who accept
the way of war on occasion as a dire but necessary last
resort in international relationship, unless we recognize
that the Christian objection is not to the *purpose* which
impels good men to war but to the *method* by which
that purpose is expressed; for the one contradicts the
other. The Christian man professes to be governed in
all things by loyalty to the purpose of Jesus Christ; and
that purpose can be stated, if in a single word, by the
word " redemption." That is, Jesus sought — here in
this world — to overcome the evil in men and to make
them at-one with the life of God. To this end, however,
— as has been pointed out in the chapter on the Author-

---

[1] Dr. Harry Emerson Fosdick of New York.

ity of Christ — his method varied with circumstance,
but was always an expression of his purpose. Thus, on
occasion he used persuasion where persuasion was an
appropriate weapon; at other times he used invective
of the severest order; sometimes he dealt with the evildoer in tenderness, or at other times his sole resort was
prayer; while on at least one occasion that is recorded
he did not disdain the use of physical force. But always, whatever means he used, he never foreclosed the
possibility of " redeeming " the men and women with
whom he was in contact.

This redemptive purpose of Jesus found its supreme
expression in Gethsemane and on the cross. There in
the Garden he definitely refused to return injury for
injury; so also he forbade his disciples to meet force with
force, not because the use of force was wrong in itself,
but because the force then available — the power of the
sword — could not be used redemptively; hence his
word to Peter: " Put up thy sword into its place." Moreover, on the cross he endured without resentment or
retaliation all that the sin of man inflicted, and persistently he gave love for hate, good for ill, blessing for
cursing; and this method was adopted in the faith
that only so could the hearts of men be touched into
response and their ill will transformed into good will.
Also it is to be observed that Jesus was not concerned
with himself alone: others were dependent on him for
safety, and the very faith which he had founded was in
jeopardy if he succumbed. He even forewarned his
followers of suffering, persecution, martyrdom, death,

which should fall upon the innocent "for his sake" in a world which had not renounced the way of the sword. Yet, even so, he never raised a finger to prevent the catastrophes which he foresaw; for to do so would have been to forsake his chosen way of redemption and to employ weapons incongruous with the way of God's love.

Other methods than his might (or might not) have prevented the evil *acts* of men, but only the method of Jesus could reach the evil *will* from which all evil acts proceed. No Christian man or woman will question that the story of the centuries has been a vindication of Christ's method in dealing with the world's evil; for explain it as we will, the gospel of the cross has reconciled man to God and man to his neighbor when other methods, and especially the method of war, have merely embittered and alienated and issued in disaster. It was so in the year A.D. 70, when the Jews rejected Christ's way of peace and chose instead to wage a "righteous war" against the Roman oppressor; and it has been so in every century since.

The Christian objection to war therefore is this, that its methods and spirit — though not necessarily its purpose — are opposed to the methods and spirit of Jesus. Can it seriously be contended, for instance, that poison-gas, high explosives, air-raids, naval blockades, torpedoes, submarines, stabbing, drowning, mutilating, shooting, or starving the "enemy," are instruments by which Christ's redemptive love is mediated to our fellow man, woman, or child?

It is not questioned that we may (though equally we may not!) by such means save our own compatriots from suffering and physical disaster; but that is not the issue. Can we by such means love the " enemy " — the personalities who together constitute the "enemy" state — into repentance? Are the several units who compose the "enemy" thereby redeemed from their enmity and made at-one with God and their foes? For nothing less than that fulfills the purpose of God for the Christian man, and nothing else can re-establish the violated "righteousness of God " by restoring right relationships among men.

It is admittedly not easy to find ways and means of instituting and maintaining these right relationships, especially after war has broken out, and this difficulty will be considered in a subsequent chapter. But at least it is obvious that war itself is not a remedy but an aggravation. The determination to meet and overcome embattled evil registers the Christian's faith in righteousness; but to meet it by the methods of war is not to vindicate righteousness, but the reverse; for it merely adds one set of evils to another, and attempts the impossible task of casting out Beelzebub by the prince of the devils. So the Christian objection to war is not to be construed as moral indifference in a struggle between right and wrong, but only as a recognition that the righteousness of God cannot be achieved by means which disallow right relationships among men. Christian pacifism is not passivity; it is the active substitution all along the line of the spirit of Christ for the spirit of war; and therefore, as with him, the giving of good for ill, right for wrong, love for hate, blessing for cursing. It is because war makes this impossible that it comes under the ban of many consciences which are nevertheless not yet clear as to an alternative duty.

The pacifist is often accused of making too much of the fact of bloodshed; but that is to misunderstand his protest. Christianity began in bloodshed: but it was the blood of the Redeemer, not the blood of the enemy. Death therefore is not a disaster from the Christian standpoint; the soldier (or the civilian) who dies in war is not thereby beyond the mercy of God or at variance with his purpose: but what of the one who kills, or who urges others to the dreadful task? The act of dying may have a redemptive efficacy; but can the act of killing? Is it not true to say that killing — like all short cuts to moral ends — is a hasty evasion of Christian responsibility? That is to say, killing does not even attempt to solve the knotty problem of meeting and overcoming evil; it merely pushes the problem off on to the hands of God!

Why do the imprecatory Psalms offend the Christian conscience? There is no literature extant which breathes so accurately the very spirit of a " just and righteous war "; but can we at one and the same moment curse the enemy and love him? The same insuperable contradiction emerges if we bring the methods and processes of war to the test of prayer " in the name of Jesus Christ." Suppose that the actual methods — and not only the exalted purpose — of a defen-

sive war for some high end were made a matter of
Christian prayer; suppose those who prayed actually
envisaged what war means in terms of blood and tears
and immorality and slanderous falsehood and calculated
ill will; could Christian people continue to approve and
support these things in the name of him who died that
his enemies might live? The answer cannot be in
doubt; for we cannot, in the name of the Savior of
mankind, pray for the destruction of men and the violation of human fellowship.

At the time of the Spanish-American War, Mark
Twain, in an article in the *Philadelphia Forum* maga-
zine, satirized the unconscious denial of Christian faith
which is always involved in a prayer for victory: such
prayers indeed are only possible because Christian people lose sight of the actual processes of war in their
devotion to the cause for which the war is fought.
Mark Twain pictured the young recruits marching to
war, and then the assembly of their elders in the church,
where the minister utters a prayer for the triumph of
the nation's armies: he puts into words the unspoken,
and the unthought of, implications of every prayer for
victory; and this is what he says:

" O Lord our Father, our young patriots, idols of our
hearts, go forth to battle — be Thou near them! With
them, in spirit, we also go forth from the sweet peace of
our beloved firesides to smite the foe. O Lord our God,
help us to tear their soldiers to bloody shreds with our
shells; help us to cover their smiling fields with the pale

forms of their patriot dead; help us to drown the thunder of the guns with the cries of the wounded, writhing in pain; help us to lay waste their humble homes with a hurricane of fire; help us to wring the hearts of their unoffending widows with unavailing grief; help us to turn them out roofless with their little children to wander unfriended through wastes of their desolated land in rags and hunger and thirst, sport of the sun-flames of summer and the icy winds of winter, broken in spirit, worn with travail, imploring Thee for the refuge of the grave and denied it; for our sakes, who adore Thee, Lord, blast their hopes, blight their lives, protract their bitter pilgrimage, make heavy their steps, water their way with tears, stain the white snow with the blood of their wounded feet! We ask of One who is the Spirit of love, and who is the ever-faithful refuge and friend of all that are sore beset, and seek His aid with humble and contrite hearts. Grant our prayer, O Lord, and Thine shall be the praise and honor and glory now and ever. Amen."

Every Christian man and woman will feel that there is something blasphemous about a prayer like that: yet it understates rather than overstates the realities of war; for it takes no account of the wartime activities of the home front. To be complete, it ought to seek God's blessing upon lying and slander, hate and ill will, cruel intolerance in thought and deed. All this and more is implied by a prayer for victory. Then why not use such a prayer? Is it not because we know that we cannot use the name of Jesus Christ for things like that? All of which means that the method of war and the method of Jesus are in irreconcilable conflict; to choose the one is to discard the other. The antithesis indeed may be stated in several ways. The way of war is destructive, of Christ redemptive; war seeks to overcome evil by the infliction of injury on the evildoer or his agents, Jesus on the cross by the endurance of the utmost injury that the evildoer cares to inflict; war treats men as things, Jesus always treated them as living souls capable of responding to the love of God; he sought to kill the enmity where war operates by killing the enemy; Jesus lost the battle in order to win men, while war crushes men in order to achieve victory.

The antithesis, when thus stated, is so plain that the task of justification lies with those who accept war as within the sanctions of Christianity rather than with those who reject it. In other words, the authority of Christ and the nature of war are so diametrically opposed that the Christian apologist for war is of necessity involved in a fatal contradiction; in the very act of justification he is bound to deny the very faith he affirms.

CHAPTER VI

SOME OF THE DIFFICULTIES OF THE CHRISTIAN POSITION

THESE difficulties have already been indicated in the chapter which stated the problem, and an endeavor must now be made to meet them. The chief of these difficulties arises from the seeming impossibility, in time of war, of prescribing any exact alternative that is not merely supine and inert.

The question was sometimes angrily put to the Christian pacifist during the World War: " What would you do if you saw a ruffian assaulting your mother? " — to which the apt retort was once made, " I don't know, but I would not go to France to shoot his uncle! " The intrinsic absurdity of war as a method of solving our dilemmas could not be better expressed. But the retort does not meet the demand of the critic for action that is positive and not merely negative; for even if it be admitted that the way of war is not a Christian reaction to aggressive evil in its assault upon the life of the nation, yet a policy of " do-nothing " is equally un-Christian in that it allows evil to have its own way and to triumph without let or hindrance over that which is good. Such for instance seemed to be the case in 1914, when men felt themselves caught in a moral dilemma which led multitudes to choose war as the lesser of two evils. It is necessary to recognize that, *for those who have not accepted the Christian way,* such a position has a large measure of validity: right and wrong are eternal and absolute values implicit in the very nature of the world, but our knowledge of things absolute is conditioned by the exercise of our fallible human judgment; and hence, in one sense, right and wrong are relative to our own degree of enlightenment. That is to say, that is right *for us* (though not for anyone else) which we feel to be right at any given moment: wider experience or greater knowledge, or the recognition of other moral standards, may alter our conception of what is right; but until such enlargement of vision occurs, we can do no other as honest men than act upon the vision we already possess. Thus, for instance, so long as men felt slavery to be right (and they did, however incredible it seems to us), they were not to be condemned or censured for holding human beings as chattels; but the moment they awoke to the Christian conception of man as no longer a " thing " to be bought and sold, but a child of God to be respected, then for them the enslavement of their fellows was wrong. The same is true of participation in or the endorsement of war: if a man has not seized the significance of the Christian reaction to aggressive evil as seen in the way of Jesus Christ, it is better to react by the way of war than not to react at all: war in such a case is relatively right for that man. So for a sub-Christian world in general: if it is not aware of any other way than war for meeting embattled evil, it cannot register its moral recoil against evil except by giving battle. In that sense, for the vast majority of people in every land in 1914, war was the " lesser of two evils," and *for them* it was right to fight: to have refrained because of cowardice or self-interest would have been a glaring dereliction of duty in face of a pressing·need.

The problem we are considering, however, is not that of a sub-Christian world which has not yet grasped the significance of the Christian way, but that of the Christian man or woman who has already seen the radical opposition between the authority of Christ and the nature of war. Can he or she reconcile the irreconcilable by pleading the world's dilemma of a choice between two evils? Such a plea is, on the face of it, a serious indictment of the providential ordering of the world. On such grounds, for instance, Herod might have justified his murder of John the Baptist, and in a similar way most of the crimes of history could be approved. But no Christian need be caught in such a dilemma; for there is always an exit from a choice of evils by the way of the cross or its equivalent, if only men have sufficient faith to take it. Compromise with the truth is the only fatal and final disloyalty. But there is never disloyalty in compulsory inertia when the way of active fidelity is closed. Consider the concrete case of 1914 as it presented itself to the people of Great Britain. The dilemma appeared to be either war or failure to honor the moral (and treaty) obligations in regard to Belgium, wantonly attacked by Germany.

But a deeper and longer view would have revealed the fact that the real menace to Belgian life lay, not in German aggression, but in something of which Germany at that moment was the supreme type and exponent, namely, men's belief in the legitimacy of armed force. Hence the truest defense, not only of Belgium but of all states, big and little, is to refuse to sanction such menacing beliefs and to give them no countenance in action. Such refusal may expose the objector to persecution, or in the last resort to martyrdom; but such martyrdom, especially if an entire community were involved in it, would inevitably stir the conscience of mankind, and mark the beginning of the end of war. This suggestion of the redemptive efficacy of a martyrdom was finely worked out by Dr. Alexander Mackennal in his Presidential Address to the Free Church Council of England and Wales at Sheffield during the Boer War in the year 1900. He said: " The hardest lesson we have to learn is that a nation which would fulfil the perfect law of Christ may have to give its life for its testimony. For many years the thought has pressed upon me that, if England is to fulfil her noblest destiny, she may be called to be a sacrificial nation; and I have had the dream that the sacrifice might be in the cause of peace. If England, in the plenitude of her power, should lay down every weapon of a carnal warfare, disband her armies, call her fleets from the seas, throw open her ports, and trust for her continued existence only to the service she could render to the world and the testimony she would bear to Christ, what would happen? I know not. . . . It might be that Christ . . . would declare that the purpose of such a sacrifice was sufficient, that the example would be enough, and that the nation would continue to be, living and strong in the gratitude of all peoples. But if otherwise, what then? Such a martyrdom would quicken the conscience of the world. . . . And of this I am sure: so long as the vision of a nation martyred for Christ's sake appears absurd and impossible, there will never be a Christian nation. This also I believe, that until our advocates of peace apprehend that such a martyrdom may be within the counsel of God, their advocacy will lack its final inspiration and its victorious appeal."

The contention of Dr. Mackennal, that readiness to suffer martyrdom for the sake of peace would spell the doom of war, may of course be questioned: it is a prediction born of faith in the divine order, and assumes — what after all is implicit in every Christian witness — that those who dare the way of the cross are bound to succeed. But, whether this faith be endorsed or rejected, it at least disposes of the plea that the Christian man must sometimes choose between war and dishonor. Jesus believed that in the struggle with moral evil the way of the cross was more potent than the way of the sword; and his followers therefore are justified in finding a similar escape from their dilemmas.

Even, however, if the Christian exit from the dilemma be not accepted, it is nevertheless a colossal assumption to suggest that war is necessarily the lesser of two evils, even though the alternative evil consists in the breach of some honorable obligation. War itself flourishes upon dishonor, broken treaties, violated promises, lies, deception, and every kind of meanness, deliberately organized into a system; so that when we are told to choose war as the lesser of two evils, we are asked to honor one promise by allowing the violation of innumerable others. This is surely hardly a convincing reason for failure to abide by the Christian way. Admittedly there is a dilemma; but it is only by a Christian reaction to the situation that both evils are transcended and both horns of the dilemma escaped.

Sometimes a justification for war is found in the coercive functions of the state: force, it is said, is the final sanction of all state action, and therefore to deny the legitimacy of war (by which the state seeks to preserve itself from external aggression) is to deny to the state any place in a Christian world-economy. Such a plea fails to recognize that even behind the state's exercise of force there is always the power of public opinion, and that the final sanction of all ordered communal life is consent and not coercion. We see this, for instance, whenever a government which has lost the confidence of the people continues to carry on the administration. This was the case in Ireland prior to the grant of its dominion status: " all the king's horses and all the king's men " were unable to give currency to the king's writ, when it was not endorsed by the consent of the populace. The same fact accounts for the periodic anarchy in backward states like the Central American Republics: coercion is not lacking, but without the consent of the governed, ordered national life is impossible.

Even if it were true however that the ultimate foundation of ordered national life is the power to coerce, it does not therefore follow that the Christian citizen must acknowledge the legitimacy of that particular form of coercion which is represented by warfare between nations. Such a process of reasoning makes the alleged well-being of the state the prime consideration (*salus populi suprema est lex*), and thereby exalts political considerations above spiritual ones: it is to appeal from Christ to Machiavelli and to make personality subordinate to nationality. But such a process means a complete inversion of our Christian judgment.

The state — like many other human institutions (the family, for instance) — comes out of human necessity and in that sense is divinely ordained; but in the Christian scheme of things all earthly institutions and relationships are subordinate to the supreme relationship of the soul to God, as seen and understood in the Person of Jesus Christ. To deny the legitimacy of war, therefore, from a Christian standpoint is not to exclude the life of the state from our consideration, any more than to deny the legitimacy of dueling is to ignore the life of the individual; it is but to affirm that there are certain state activities (as there are individual activities) which a Christian judgment cannot endorse. Jesus did not deny the legitimacy of family life when he said that under certain circumstances a man may have to " hate " his father and mother; and so with the state. What is and what is not permissible to the state, in a Christian sense, cannot in every detail be determined *a priori;* all that can be done, therefore, is to consider each particular case as it arises. The state at war — or contemplating war — lays certain demands upon its citizens, and such demands (like all else in human life) must be checked by the Christian and either accepted or rejected, not according to some preconceived theory of the state, but only in the light of the authority of Christ.

Much of the difficulty here arises from confusing an army with a police force, to which reference has already been made. When we see a policeman apprehending a recalcitrant citizen and coercing him in the name of the state, it is easy to assume the right of the state to deal by force of arms with a recalcitrant nation which adopts aggressive tactics toward its neighbors. But such an assumption rests upon a false analogy, and it is this which misleads us. It has already been pointed out that, in certain vital respects, the *methods* of an army and those of a police force are fundamentally at variance; but this is also true in regard to the respective *objects* of military and police activity. If the argument assumed an international authority, dealing impartially with disputing states by means of warlike operations, the analogy with a civil police force would be nearer the mark; but even then it would be inaccurate, for it presumes an equation between the community which needs to be held in check and the individual citizen who may have to be coerced. This equation, however, cannot be established, if we get beneath purely superficial similarities. An individual citizen differs from a nation in two respects which make any exact parallel between them impossible: an individual is a unit, and if he is bent on unsocial action, he can be dealt with as a single wrongdoer; but a nation is a complex entity and never acts as a consolidated unit: within every nation, that is to say, there are diverse elements, some bad and some good, some bent on action inconsistent with international harmony, and some opposed to such action, some militarist and some pacific. A further difference between an individual and a nation is found in the fact that the former is mobile and the latter is not: a citizen can change his place of residence, he can evade the arm of the law by movement within the country, by hiding himself, or by " leaving his country for his country's good ": but a nation, as such, has no power of movement, it is fixed within certain known territorial limits, and it therefore can neither be hidden nor can it escape the reach of international law by stepping out of the community of nations into another planet where the writ of civilization does not run. All this means that the methods which may be appropriate and effective in dealing with an individual cannot, by the nature of the case, be applied in dealing with a nation. It is quite obvious, for instance, that a nation cannot be arrested or placed behind prison bars,[1] nor, even were it feasible, is it necessary. For, since a nation is a

---

1 The ancients actually did something of this kind when a people was taken into captivity, as with the Jews in Babylon; but the numbers were inconsiderable compared with modern communities, and economic considerations in a highly industrialized world make any such process impossible today.

composite and complex entity, we act in defiance of the facts if we treat it or think of it as a consolidated unit, unanimously playing the part of an international criminal. Yet this is what war always does: the whole of the opposing nation is " the enemy," and no distinction is drawn between the diverse and often conflicting elements within it. If, however, account be taken of this diversity it will be seen that there is a better and more effective way of dealing with a " criminal nation " than by the act of war: for it is always possible, by a generous and humane foreign policy, to encourage the liberal and pacific elements in another nation and to discourage the predatory and militarist elements. In this way any alleged " criminal " intentions are rendered impotent, not by coercion from outside, but by restraint from within the frontiers. An appeal can be made from " Philip drunk to Philip sober."

A simple instance will illustrate. In 1838 the United States and Canada were on the brink of war, on account of the activities of groups of smugglers and raiders on the American side (known as hunters' lodges), who hoped thus to provoke a rebellion in Canada which would secure the inclusion of the dominion (as it has since become) in the American Union. Fortunately for both countries, there were statesmen in Canada who kept their heads under this provocation. Instead, therefore, of replying to the American raids by a declaration of war, they sent an embassy to Washington and induced the non-hostile elements in the United States to deal with the unfriendly action by rousing public opinion against it, and by police action (in the proper sense) on the American side of the border. The fact, already noted, that war in the modern world is always justified in the name of " defense " gives to this type of appeal more weight than ever before. For no statesman bent upon aggressive designs toward a neighbor nation could possibly induce his people to believe that he was proposing a war of defense, so long as the policy of the other nation was obviously peaceable and reasonable and friendly, and not accompanied by the mobilization of armed forces or threats of war. Indeed, press the matter far enough, and it is possible to say that a nation which dared to be completely disarmed would be completely safe from the menace of war; for there could be no need to defend one's country from an unarmed foe, and the argument of defense by which warmakers must perforce disguise their designs would be paralyzed at the outset. The plea, therefore, that war is a justifiable activity for the Christian, because by it alone can the state preserve itself from external aggression, is invalid not only because it ignores the authority of Christ, but even in the light of political fact and the expediencies of statecraft.

It is in connection with the state that many people find another difficulty in the Christian position; for our citizenship is a fact which is intimately associated with the fact of war. The citizen may be a Christian man, but he is also one of the units which compose the state; and this relationship is therefore often alleged as a justification for participation in war. The position may be stated as follows: The individual cannot contract out of privileges and obligations which are due to his membership of the group (be it family or society or nation) to which he belongs; the individual conscience, therefore, must be subordinate to the common weal; and hence, when the state goes to war, the citizen — whatever his private convictions — must acquiesce and co-operate! Such a plea, however, rests upon a false opposition; for there is in fact no such thing as an isolated individual: he is always a social unit, and both his rights and his duties are derived from his relationship to his social context. But that context is not fully comprehended by our citizenship or our place in the state: it is thus not putting the matter correctly when conscience is represented as individualistic, and as therefore in conflict with the corporate responsibilities of citizenship. The position is only indicated truly when it is recognized that, while I am a citizen of the state, I am also a member of the church, and a unit in the social-spiritual entity which Jesus called the Kingdom of Heaven: I am a child of earth and also a child of God. Then what am I to do if the demands of Cæsar conflict with the demands of Christ? Suppose two or more social loyalties clash, which, then, is to take precedence? What is it which — in the view of the apologist for war — gives to the state its super-moral right to override the Christian way? And if loyalty to the state may qualify my allegiance to Christ, why may not loyalty to my social class, or my trade union, or my family, or my church, or any other group of which I happen to be a member?

The New Testament at least gives no undecided answer:
" We must obey God rather than men," which means
that I must choose the wider loyalty, *knowing that in
the long run the wider welfare will always include the
narrower*. That is to say, it is my duty to act as a Christian to the limit of my power, to refuse any method but
that of Jesus Christ, and whatever others feel *their* duty
to be, be true to mine and leave the consequences in the
hands of God. When that principle is applied to the
case of war, the logical issue is pacifism, a refusal to engage in or to endorse the methods of war. The apostles
faced the same issue when, in defiance of magisterial
demands which conflicted with the authority of Christ,
they chose the will of God before the behests of the state.
D'Alembert, the French mathematician, indicated the
ascending scale of loyalties which bind the Christian
man, in the statement, " I prefer my family to myself, I
prefer my country to my family, I prefer Humanity to
my country." There is no good citizen who would not
subscribe to the first two clauses of this statement; but
if these are incontrovertible and axiomatic from a Christian standpoint, so is the final clause. My deepest good
can never be secured by the sacrifice of my family to
my personal interests, and the same is true of the subordination of my country to my family: it is not a matter of dispute, and need not therefore be argued, that
the welfare of the greater always includes the welfare
of the less, even though in the process the lesser group
outwardly suffers. But the same holds true when a
Christian man, in loyalty to the Kingdom of Heaven,

refuses to obey the behest of the state in going to war: in such refusal he is not putting a narrowly personal preference against the claims of society: he is serving the earthly society by seeking to raise it to the level of the heavenly. James Russell Lowell asserted this truth when he resisted the demand of the American Republic on a critical occasion:

We owe allegiance to the State, but deeper, truer, more,
To the sympathies which God hath set within our spirits'
    core;
Our country claims our fealty: we grant it so; but then,
Before Man made us citizens, great Nature made us
    men.[2]

Many people are misled by what seems to them the impersonal aspect of war. It may be admitted that to act " redemptively " is the Christian way in relationships which involve personal dealings; but a large proportion of our normal activities are not on this plane: they are not concerned with the " redemption " of men, and are properly described from a moral point of view as neutral: as such they are neither Christian nor unChristian. The purchase of a postage-stamp, for instance, from an employee whom we never saw before and may never meet again. It is, of course, true that many of the operations of war are equally impersonal, and it is therefore possible to argue that they have nothing to do with the authority of Christ. But, when

[2] James Russell Lowell in " Fugitive Slaves."

our action affects the very life of our fellow creatures so intimately and so disastrously as does our action in war, have we any right as Christians to act in this detached and impersonal way? It is the old question: " Am I my brother's keeper? " The purchase of a postage-stamp is in no way a violation of Christian relationship, and it does not stand athwart " redemptive " activity, if the occasion for such should arise. The common conscience of Christian men, however, condemns the deliberate purchase of " sweated goods," however impersonal the relationship between buyer and seller, because behind the impersonal transaction is the infliction of injury upon some person or persons unknown: we recognize there that impersonal contacts cannot cancel the Christian's responsibility. He may not be able to act in a directly " redemptive " way toward the victims of the social order; but the authority of Christ bids him refrain from anything which intensifies the ill or gives it sanction. The same principle applies in regard to the many impersonal operations of war: they none of them have the innocuous quality which belongs to the purchase of a postage-stamp; but they are all of them accessory to a system which, in its methods and processes, is always a flagrant defiance of the authority of Christ.

Much of the hesitation which men feel in refusing the way of war arises from a fear of what may follow upon such refusal. It seems as though disaster, spiritual as well as physical, must necessarily ensue unless resistance be made to the assault of aggressive evil; and hence it is said to be our duty to conserve the moral values embodied in the state, by resisting the aggression which would destroy those values. Incidentally, such an argument ignores the fact that all moral values go by the board in the act of war; and we therefore smite the very thing we desire to preserve whenever we resort to arms for the maintenance of moral values. Such values, indeed, can neither be destroyed nor maintained by physical weapons, but only as men are either false to them or faithful to them as the case may be. Spiritual things can be attacked or defended only by spiritual means. Was Christianity destroyed when Jesus was crucified? Also it can be pointed out that this plea for armed defense for the maintenance of moral values postulates, not merely the necessity of resistance, but of *successful* resistance, which a recourse to war can never promise. Apart, however, from such an assumption, if the way and spirit of Jesus are to be our guide, such considerations are, strictly speaking, an irrelevance. The result of speaking the truth seems in certain cases, and when judged by a narrow pragmatic test, to be disastrous; but all truth goes by the board if once it is admitted that falsehood is morally justified. As a matter of fact, the ultimate far-reaching effects of any human act can never be entirely foreseen; we have to act in faith, and as Christians our faith rests upon our knowledge of Jesus Christ. Christian morality is neither pragmatic nor utilitarian in the sense that we can try it out and judge it by its works. The acceptance of the Christian standard rests upon the faith that God, seeing the beginning and the end of every human deed as we cannot, and understanding the ultimate effects of every smallest act as no finite mind can do, yet deliberately chose the way of the cross and rejected the way of the sword as the only effective way of combatting the world's evil. In that faith, therefore, since the way of war and the way of the cross are antithetical, the Christian is called to repudiate the methods of the battlefield.

That the difficulties of the Christian position are many and serious is obvious enough; but every endeavor to find a Christian apologia for war fails if we keep the authority of Christ in the center. When or under what provocation, or in what dilemma, or for what reasons, did Jesus ever allow his followers to depart from his redemptive method? Did he ever admit directly or by implication that the end justifies the means, or that Christian obligations are canceled when a Christian acts as the agent of a group? The burden of proof, therefore, lies with those who justify war in the name of Christ, and not with those who condemn it. For pacifism after all is but one application of the gospel method; it is Christ's way of meeting evil, applied to the supreme evil of international conflict. If Christianity must be qualified or jettisoned in favor of war, it is not a gospel of redemption but only a second-best. But if when war comes Christianity can meet embattled and organized evil by pointing a better way, then — though the church which bears the Christian witness may be crucified and martyred — the way of Jesus Christ will stand before the world as verily in every emergency "the power of God unto salvation."

CHAPTER VII

THE CHRISTIAN WITNESS IN A WORLD ORGANIZED FOR WAR

MAN has been described as a " gregarious animal," and that native and God-ordained fact lies at the basis of all human association, whether in the nation, in the church, in commercial or cultural organizations, or in any other department of human life. The state is the nation organized for political purposes, and it exists in order to give effect to the right ordering of human life. In this sense the Apostle Paul, speaking of the Roman imperium, declares that " the powers that be are ordained of God "; though it is to be noted that not many years later, when those powers had begun to persecute the Christians, they were referred to in the Book of the Revelation in anything but divine terms: to the writer of that book, indeed, the Roman State was the " harlot " and the emperor was the " beast." The distinctive character of the state lies in its power to enforce its authority, and therein it differs from the other associations of human life with which we are familiar. The church or the trade union may excommunicate, but under modern conditions the power to coerce belongs only to the state; and it is when that power is exercised, not upon its own citizens but toward another state, that we have a condition of war. The League of Nations is, in effect, a super-state within limits which it is hoped will ultimately become world-wide; and it is inevitable that, in the course of political development, the sovereign state as we know it will surrender its right to make war in favor of the judicial and legislative authority of the League or some other world organization. In the meantime, however, the Christian man, as has been pointed out in the previous chapter, may find that as a citizen of an earthly state organized for war he is called to do that which violates his duty as a churchman or as a citizen of the Kingdom of Heaven.

How, then, in such circumstances shall he make his Christian witness? First, it has to be recognized that Christianity does not spell anarchy. If the state is not a divine institution in the old sense of the " divine right of kings," at least order and an organized social economy are a necessary condition of a full and free and disciplined Christian life; and therefore the Christian citizen will give his loyalty and support wherever possible to the authority of the government under which he lives. But there is a limit to such loyalty; and that limit is reached when obedience to the state clashes with fidelity to something that is greater: as Christians we are to " render to Cæsar the things that are Cæsar's, and to God the things that are God's."

This has been the principle upon which Christian men have acted all down the ages. An apt statement of this principle was made by one of the ejected ministers under the Act of Uniformity in England in 1662, and his words are strictly relevant to the subject of this chapter: they were spoken by Robert Atkins in his farewell sermon from the pulpit of Exeter Cathedral: " Let him never be accounted a sound Christian who does not fear God and honor the king. I beg you will not interpret our nonconformity to be an act of unpeaceableness and disloyalty. We will do everything for His Majesty but sin: we will hazard everything for him but our souls: we hope we could die for him if the need arose, but we dare not and we will not be damned for him! "

We today should not use the idiom of this seventeenth-century Christian; but he puts his finger upon a salient consideration when he indicates that it is only with grave reluctance and with deep distress of soul that the Christian man can thus set himself in opposition to the demands of the state. This is especially so when the state itself is in danger from an enemy who is waging war; for the call to arms is after all the world's way — and the only way the world knows — of meeting embattled evil; and the Christian man therefore cannot be content with a mere negative which contracts out of the strife — even were that wholly possible — or which has no concern for the welfare of the state of which he is a citizen.

Then how is a Christian witness to be made in a world either actually at war, or organized for war, as are all the great nations of today? What is the Christian's alternative to war? Experience during the World War showed how difficult it is, when once battle is joined, to find a positive way of serving the state apart from warlike activity or some occupation auxiliary to war: the power of the state practically prohibited every effort but that of the soldier and those who supplied his needs, and the universal motto was " Get on with the war."

The obvious alternative to settling an international dispute by fighting is to settle it by negotiation. This, however, is not an alternative which is at the disposal of the individual Christian. He may, of course, plead for such an alternative, and seek to influence public opinion in that direction; but the populace is not likely to respond to his appeal; for, inflamed by the passions which war engenders, the people generally regard the mere suggestion of negotiating with the enemy as disloyalty to their own country; while the statesmen, pledged by secret treaties to aims which can only be realized by victory, readily encourage this attitude of unreason. This was seen again and again during the World War. The editor of the *Venturer,* for instance, in 1917, at Bow Street Police Court, in London, was fined $250 or, in default of payment, committed to jail under a sentence of three months' hard labor, for the " crime " of criticizing the British government's refusal to negotiate at what seemed to be a favorable moment. The actual charge was laid under the Defense of the Realm Act as one of " prejudicing the discipline of His Majesty's forces "; but the issue in court was an article condemning the policy of His Majesty's government; for the court held that the words used were " likely " to subvert the will to fight both among soldiers and civilians. In this and other ways political criticism was stifled; printers were prosecuted or their machinery dismantled if they dared to print " peace literature "; organizations which carried on propaganda for peace had their offices raided and their material seized; and lessees of public halls were given to understand that it was inadvisable to let their premises for peace meetings. As a result the protagonists of " peace by negotiation " found themselves stultified and condemned to political impotence.

When it is borne in mind that war arises only after the breakdown of negotiations, it is not surprising that there should be popular impatience with a demand to substitute negotiation for fighting. Indeed, whatever may be the case as the conflict proceeds, it is true that at the outset of a war " peace by negotiation " is not practical politics; and it is this inability to find a positive alternative to war which leads many Christian people to feel that their highest duty lies in a heavyhearted and yet wholehearted support of military operations, as the one and only way of registering their Christian abhorrence of, and reaction to, the aggressive evil which threatens the nation's life.

This dilemma still plays a large part in the support accorded to war and warlike preparations by Christian people who love peace and seek it with passionate conviction: they do not justify war in its methods and processes as a Christian reaction to evil; but still less Christian is it to make no reaction at all; and so they challenge the out-and-out opponent of war to prescribe his Christian alternative — if he can!

Before endeavoring to meet this challenge, the demand itself must be scrutinized, and we must understand just what is implied by it. As generally presented, the demand means not that the individual Christian shall find some positive alternative to the activity of the soldier, but that he shall prescribe a definite and regimented alternative for all who are opposed to war. Thus during the World War the conscientious objector was not, except in a few rare cases, allowed to continue in the vocation for which he had been trained or in which he had experience, and so serve his country by the faithful performance of a task for which he was fitted. The wartime temper insisted that since the soldier made a sacrifice, the man of peace must do the same. So if he was a schoolmaster, he was set to dig potatoes; if he was a professor of economics, he was told to dress wounds in an out-patient department of a civil hospital; if he was an agricultural laborer he was expected to break stones for road repairs; and if he felt that a Christian man ought to direct his own life under God, and not at the command of men, he was sent to prison and kept in solitary confinement for years on end, lest he should contaminate a war-mad community by his fidelity to conscience.[1]

But the very demand for a regimented alternative to

---

[1] Absurd as some of these instances seem, every one of them occurred as part of the normal treatment of conscientious objectors during the war. See *Conscription and Conscience,* by John W. Graham, for particulars.

soldiering reveals, not a Christian standpoint, but the trail of the military mind. There is regimentation for war — so runs the argument, implicitly if not explicitly — and therefore there ought to be regimentation for peace. So the Christian is challenged to show how, in time of war, citizens can be enrolled for national service in some civilian organization, which shall thus provide a definite alternative to enrolment in the military forces; and if the opponent of war cannot meet this challenge his case is assumed to lack its final and convincing support.

It is to the very terms of this challenge however that objection must be taken on Christian grounds; for it is neither true to the genius of the gospel nor to the facts of Christian experience to suggest, as this challenge does, that there is one specific and definite way in which an opponent of war should react to a national crisis. On the contrary, the glory of the Christian way is its freedom under the control of the Spirit of God: " the wind bloweth where it listeth . . . and so is every one that is born of the Spirit "; therefore, by the nature of the case, a stereotyped and regimented alternative to war is something which no man has a right to demand of another. There are, indeed — in regard to a national crisis, as in regard to every other — as many Christian reactions as there are Christian people: each one will make a different reaction because of his different outlook or circumstance, or his consciousness of the divine leading for his particular life. All, therefore, that anyone has a right to demand of a professedly Christian

man is that he shall live a Christian life to the extent
of his power, and await the event and the opportunity
in determining how his Christianity will find expression in a given crisis.

From the beginning of the Christian era it has been
true that the world has never been able to predict how
a Christian would act. It was so with Jesus himself:
men were continually baffled by the unexpected in
him; the Pharisees prescribed definite ways in which a
religious man would act, but in the freedom of the
Spirit Jesus ignored their narrow prescriptions and
went his own way in obedience to the will of God. It
has been the same with the followers of Jesus in every
age, and it is still so today. Obedience to the will of
God may on occasion demand an active and vigorous
response to the assault of evil: it was so when Jesus
retorted with vehemence to the " hypocrisy " of the
Pharisees, or when he evaded the mob at Nazareth, or
when in the Garden of Gethsemane he stood across the
path of the armed guards in order that his disciples
might go free. But equally, on occasion, obedience to
the will of God may require quiescence in the face of
aggressive evil: this was the case when Jesus met the
evil designs of Pharisees and Herodians by quietly moving across the Jordan, where he would be beyond the
power of his persecutors; or most plainly of all, when
he was silent before Herod, and unresisting in those last
hours which took him to the cross. We must therefore
not rule out as a possible Christian reaction in time of
war a policy which *outwardly* may be described as " do

nothing." " They also serve who only stand and wait ";
and sometimes the self-restraint involved in such Christian quiescence is infinitely more difficult to achieve
than the spontaneous vigor by which the " natural
man " hits back, when he or those within his care are
the victims of high-handed wrong.

Where the natural man misjudges Christian quiescence is in his assumption that it is a purely negative
attitude, and that its practical effectiveness is nil. On
such grounds the early Christian martyrs could be dismissed as negligible; for as Professor Sir William Ramsay has told us, " A little incense (on the altar of the
emperor) was nothing. An excellent and convincing
argument could readily be worked out; and then the
whole ritual of the state religion would have followed
as a matter of course: Christ and Augustus would have
been enthroned side by side . . . and everything which
was vital to Christianity would have been lost." [2]   Yet
it is a commonplace to say that it was the quiet fidelity
of the martyrs, even unto death, which won for us the
Christian privileges we possess today: no violent resistance to Roman persecution could have secured what
their silent suffering effected. Then why is a quiet refusal to wage war at the behest of a modern state to be
condemned as unworthy of a Christian man, when —
as is generally the case in wartime — all avenues of positive or active testimony for peace are closed? It is at
least obvious that, if such refusal were multiplied sufficiently, it would paralyze the arm of war; for fighting

[2] Sir William Ramsay, *Paul, the Traveller and Roman Citizen.*

cannot be conducted if one side refuses to give battle!
It is therefore not the pacifist who should be rebuked,
but the fighter; for in these days — as our analysis of
war has shown — prudence and patriotism are on the
side of pacifism; and a policy of apparent " do nothing," when war is declared, is the only way in which
civilization can be preserved from the utter disaster
which modern weapons promise to a world which is
un-Christian enough and foolish enough to fight.

The Christian position is sometimes met by the retort that, while a negative attitude may be justified
when one's own safety is endangered, yet it can never
be a Christian duty to stand idly by when the safety of
others — and particularly that of the weak and the
helpless — is menaced. But what if " do nothing " is a
more effective defense than resistance? Under modern conditions that is always the case in war; for it is
the merest make-believe to suggest that war ever can or
does defend those whose safety we desire. It has been
computed on a conservative reckoning [3] that thirteen
million civilians, of whom a vast number were women
and children, died either by violence or by starvation as
a result of the World War; in addition there were five
million war-widows and nine million orphans. By all
the forecasts a " next war " will not stop even at these
figures. It is time, therefore, that military-minded folk,
who talk of the duty of " defense " and the necessity for
a positive alternative to war, faced the realities of the

[3] *Direct and Indirect Costs of the Great World War,* by Prof. E. L.
Bogart.

situation instead of cherishing time-honored illusions. To say, as was frequently said during the World War, that a Christian man would not stand by, inert and helpless, while a bully assaulted a child, is to assume that such a situation is of the essence of war; but the assumption cannot be granted, for it is a false analogy. The practical dilemma of war lies in the fact that you cannot resist the " bully " except by killing the " child," or more truly, thirteen millions of him! To justify war therefore, because it is a Christian duty to " defend " the weak is to be the victim of unthinking sentiment and is to work untold damage. The most obvious facts negative such a plea: in 1914, for instance, Antwerp was " defended," and therefore it suffered; but Brussels, for strategic reasons, was not defended, and in consequence its inhabitants were unharmed. Similarly throughout the battle area.

If, however, the Christian duty of " defense " is still pressed, let the following incident be considered. It was reported in the *London Times* early in the course of the World War [4] that during the German advance through Belgium a party of Prussian cavalry scouts overtook a Belgian peasant, who, with his wife and three children, was flying toward France before the oncoming tide of war. The Prussians demanded certain information as to Belgian military dispositions, and as a civilian and a loyal subject of his king, the peasant re-

---

[4] The exact reference cannot be traced, but whether the incident was fact or only propaganda, no one will question the possibility of such happenings in war, and its value as an illustration does not depend upon its historicity.

fused to comply: whereupon the Prussian officer threatened that, unless the information were forthcoming,
the man's wife and children would be lined up and
shot. Will those who declare that it is always a Christian's first duty to defend the weak say what that peasant ought to have done? The *Times* praised his patriotism in sacrificing his wife and children, and in then
himself paying the extreme price of loyalty to king and
country. Thus, even on the plane of military ethics, occasions may arise when to " do nothing " is the highest
expediency and the obvious line of honor and of duty,
even though it expose the helpless to violence and death.

In the same way, then, the Christian has a King
whose will and way take precedence of the demands
of every earthly monarch; and if, in supreme loyalty to
that King, he must at times " do nothing " and seem to
be heedless of those whom he ought to defend, he is
nevertheless thereby taking the only course that is consistent with his pledged obedience to the authority of
Christ.

It is not to be concluded from this, however, that the
Christian man is shut up to the impotence of a purely
negative witness in face of the international situations
which threaten to issue in war. On the contrary, his
very refusal to engage in war, though it often adds to
the embitterment of those who do not understand it,
focuses attention upon the fundamental opposition between the authority of Christ and the way of battle, and
thereby renders a positive service. Altogether, there
were some fifteen thousand conscientious objectors un-

der the Military Service Acts in Great Britain during the World War: it is not suggested that they all took their stand on Christian grounds: far from it: the spirit and attitude of some was an exact reflection of the temper of war, and was a reproach and a hindrance to the cause of peace. But there are black sheep in every flock, and for purposes of discussion we must take both the soldier and the pacifist at his best. When every discount then has been made, it remains true that the apparently futile and negative witness of the conscientious objector struck the imagination of the world far more deeply than seemed possible at the time.

To be committed to prison instead of to the battle front seemed to the world of 1914–18 to be an inglorious response to the nation's need; and the men who languished in solitary confinement earned a contempt and a hatred from their fellow countrymen which was often more intense than that bestowed upon the " enemy." But today they have their reward in the growing recognition of the truth for which they stood: for thinking men everywhere are coming to see that the real enemy in war is not the army of the foe, but the belief — shared by friend and foe alike — that war falls within the sanctions of civilization or even of Christianity. Every man and woman, therefore, who rejects that belief, and expresses his rejection in a refusal to assist the processes of war, is playing his part far more effectively than any soldier in the real and lasting defense of his country against the enemy of mankind. If this were realized by those who complain of the " negative " at-

titude of the pacifist, they would not be so prone to
feel that when war "lets hell loose" upon the world,
the Christian's duty is to intensify that hell by his own
participation. As well say that when everybody gets
drunk I must get drunk too!

The Christian witness therefore — in spite of its seeming impotence — is one of the most vital assets for peace
in a world still organized for war. For it is obvious that
if war were renounced as the deadliest of all sins — because it includes every sin in the catalogue of vice —
then battle would become as obsolete as the duel, and
armaments would rust because of desuetude, and soldiering would be transformed into a picturesque pageantry of state, as harmless and as interesting as the
Beefeaters in the Tower of London or the Swiss Guard
which waits upon the Pope.

That fact however lays upon Christian people their
most solemn responsibility in this matter. The frenzied and unscrupulous efforts during the World War [5]
to enlist the support of the churches was evidence
enough of the value which statesmen attach to organized Christianity in time of national crisis: it was, in
fact, the biggest single factor in maintaining the war-
morale of the nation, for it enabled the public to think
of the struggle as a "holy war" and a crusade in which
it was a Christian virtue to engage.

Let the church therefore but withdraw her endorse-

---

[5] The British and American War Departments not only used eloquent
clerics as official propagandists, but sermons were prepared by war-office
clerks and circulated for use in the pulpit.

ment of war in as thoroughgoing and absolute a fashion as she would refuse to approve slavery, and the world's statesmanship would speedily discover other and better ways of dealing with international disputes than by the customary threat of armed force. It is not, of course, that statesmen desire war, or, as a rule, even threaten it openly; but diplomatic negotiations are carried on with the consciousness that armaments are in the background and to be used in cases of necessity. It is primarily a psychological situation; for the awareness of a possible appeal to war gives to diplomatic interchange a strained and anxious quality which does not belong to other relationships from which force is absent. Yet it lies within the power of the church to change the psychology of statecraft by the simple device of excommunicating war and all its works from her borders as something alien to the authority of Christ. By this is meant not merely resolutions in favor of peace, but a refusal to be used in any way by the war machine. Chaplains would disappear from the army and navy,[6] and church parades by drilled troops would be discarded as a relic of paganism — unless, indeed, the authorities were prepared to allow Christ's gospel of peace to have free course among the soldiers! To appreciate the insuperable difficulties of War-Office padres in preaching the gospel of Christ without treason to the state, one can turn to C. E. Montague's *Disenchant-*

---

[6] That is, chaplains holding military or naval commissions and therefore sworn to military obedience. Voluntary chaplaincies with entire liberty to obey the authority of Christ in ministering to the forces would be permissable to the church, though hardly likely to be permitted by the army!

ment: in every case it was the gospel that suffered and not the state-at-war, for it was hardly possible to tell a company going into a bayonet charge to "love their enemies" or to be crucified on behalf of the foe! So, too, the church would encourage and stand by her young men who, in the name of Christ, refused to obey the call to war;[7] and above all, she would refuse to break the unity of the Christian fellowship at the behest of political expediency, by dividing men and peoples into arbitrary categories of friend and foe. War is possible because statesmen can rely upon the peoples to accept certain others as their official "enemies"; but let it be known that the church will never acquiesce in this mechanical and wholesale breach of fellowship, and she would go far to paralyze the hand of war.[8] Indeed, if there should ever be a "next war," the prime

[7] Christian parents can take a stand forthwith by disallowing the enrolment of their sons in the Officers' Training Corps now established in so many of our schools: by such refusal a sentiment would speedily be created which would rob the O.T.C.'s of their social prestige.

[8] There are some who would go further than this and require of Christian citizens the refusal of war-taxation, just as they would require the refusal of military service. There is, however, a distinction to be observed here between property and personality; for the one can be seized and appropriated by government, whatever its possessor may desire, while the other can never be coerced so long as it is willing to suffer the disabilities, or worse, which a government may inflict. The payment of taxes falls in the first category, and the rendering of military service in the other: no government can compel me to shoulder a rifle or to use my labor in military preparations; but no power of mine can prevent a government from seizing my goods or raiding my bank account for the maintenance of armaments. When, therefore, I draw a cheque and hand it to the tax-collector I am merely recognizing the plain fact that I cannot control my property as I can my personality. The question of war-taxation, however, is one of the many border-line problems of Christian ethics, and in no wise affects the main issue. It has been observed that Jesus paid taxes, and yet no one would say that he endorsed Roman militarism.

responsibility for the calamity will rest with the Christian church because she did not — while yet there was time — give due warning to the world that the professed disciples of the Prince of Peace could never again be inveigled into battle. Such an attitude would doubtless bring the church under the ban of states organized for war, and members of her fellowship, as once with the church's Head, under the charge of high treason. But how can the unity of Christendom ever be asserted as more than a pious unmeaning dogma, except it be asserted in the teeth of political prohibitions? The church which is faithful to her Lord can make no terms with the mass-enmities which jeopardize her own spiritual unity with Christ's disciples everywhere. In 1914, the churches generally were taken unprepared: it was an entirely fresh issue for the majority of Christian people, and the seeming dilemma of a choice between two evils led pulpit and pew alike, for the most part, to go with the tide of popular feeling: there was no attempt or even desire to stem the tide, and the church found herself in the impotent and humiliating position of merely saying " Amen " to the speeches of the statesmen. This happened in every country which entered the war. But today we have had an opportunity, as we had not then, of knowing something of the nature of war; and by sober reflection the church has been able, if she would, to test the processes and methods of war by the authority of Christ. She knows today, as she did not in 1914, that to take the way of war is not to take the way of Christ.

Moreover, the church has at her disposal a practical substitute for war whereby she can if she will make effective her Christian reaction to aggressive and embattled evil, for the real alternative to the military way is the missionary way; and again and again the weaponless retort of a Christian life — and often of a Christian death — has proved more potent than the weapons of a sub-Christian world-order. This was the way in which Livingstone assaulted "darkest Africa": Boniface, in the eighth century, had a better idea of defeating "the Huns" than did the Allies in 1914: so, too, in the seventeenth century, William Penn showed how, in the absence of armed defense, a Christian spirit could destroy the hostility of bloodthirsty savages in Pennsylvania; in every contiguous colony "protected" by force of arms, rapine and fire and atrocity made life precarious; for seventy-two years the contrast lasted until the Quakers were outnumbered by immigrants, who insisted on a militia, and promptly one of the worst massacres in colonial history occurred on Pennsylvanian soil! Yet the world in its madness refused to learn!

Mr. Laurence Housman, the author of *The Little Plays of St. Francis,* has suggested one way in which this constructive service might be applied today to situations which contain the menace of war; and his suggestion indicates the sort of thing which the Christian conscience could endorse as a substitute for armed force. He proposes the enlistment of our young men and women in an army dedicated to the service of mankind instead of to the slaughter of our enemies. They would find all the comradeship and adventure which war offers to youth, not in fighting their fellow men but in fighting the ills which are the common lot of humanity.

For instance, one of the perpetual threats to peace in the Far East is the existence of wandering war lords and organized banditry in China. It was this fact which gave to the Japanese government its pretext for military operations in Manchuria in 1932. Few people, however, stay to ask why banditry exists; and yet the reasons are well known. Millions of people in various parts of China are the victims year by year of disastrous floods, which destroy the crops and reduce the population to starvation and beggary, and it is from this population chiefly that the swarms of bandits are drawn; the problem is perpetual so long as flood and famine recruit the ranks of desperate men. What is needed is systematic afforestation; for it is the cutting of timber and the failure to replace the forests which have led to the annual flooding of the rivers. The obvious remedy, therefore, is not to be found in military expeditions, but in the kind of missionary enterprise which will invade China with an army of helpers trained to lead and assist the people in reclaiming the flooded areas of the lowlands, and in planting millions of trees on the uplands. The military way is to shoot the bandit and leave the problem as it was; but the Christian way is to redeem the bandit by turning him into a good citizen. Suppose, then, that even a small part of the taxation now devoted to armaments were redirected into constructive channels like this — does anyone doubt that it would yield interest a hundred fold in good will between East and West?

Another center of disturbance is the Northwest Frontier of India, and from time to time we read of air-raids and other military measures for holding turbulent tribes in check. Yet another and a better way of insuring the peace of the Frontier was put into practice by an English missionary doctor named Theodore Pennell thirty years ago. With his medicine chest, he traveled alone and unarmed among the warlike tribes, ministering to the enemies of his country often at the risk of his life, until he won their confidence and affection. Indeed, so successful was he in this that he was acclaimed by a high military authority as "worth a couple of British regiments" to the peace of Northwest India. Again, therefore, it is obvious that the Christian way is more effective — even on the world's level — than the military way. Suppose, then, that the British government mobilized regiments of volunteers to construct a network of roads among the mountains, not for military but for commercial purposes; suppose that, instead of building forts, it erected hospitals; instead of barracks for British soldiers, schools for native children! Is it not clear that as a matter of practical politics (to say nothing of Christian principle) the hostile tribes would speedily become friendly, and the necessity for the armed defense of the Frontier would disappear?

One can imagine the same kind of thing being done

in Europe as in Asia. At the close of the war a group of young men — organized by the Fellowship of Reconciliation, and including British, Germans, Swiss, Americans and Italians — undertook the building of one of the shattered villages on the eastern frontier of France; they enlisted for a definite period and worked for a soldier's pay; and the village stands today as a monument to the healing power of the Christian spirit. Statesmen and people alike are slow to learn the lesson of such an incident; but the Christian man or woman who acclaims the authority of Christ will see in the multiplication of that kind of service the only effective key to European peace.

There are countless other avenues along which the energies of an organized army of peace could be directed. The tracking and charting of icebergs on the steamship routes of the North Atlantic could be undertaken on a far wider scale than at present; the visitation of lonely islands, or of the deep sea fishing fleets, could be carried out by naval units stripped of their guns and equipped with medical and other supplies; as a great city maintains its fire department and a country its lighthouse and lifeboat services, so each nation — if it were moved by Christian wisdom — would organize its expeditionary corps for service overseas, and invite the enlistment of its younger citizens, both men and women. Then, at the call of some desperate need, it would succor the victims and give the needed relief. It might be an earthquake in Japan, an area in the Near East stricken with plague or typhus, the bursting of a dam in Mesopotamia, a volcanic eruption in Sicily, a tidal wave in Mexico, a typhoon in the China Seas, or any other circumstance calling for swift action and speedy help.

In this matter of war and peace, however, the important thing is that the church should cease to be ambiguous; otherwise she will forfeit all claim to moral leadership. It is easy to plead many plausible reasons against reliance upon the Christian way when an emergency arises, and no follower of Jesus Christ, conscious of his own weakness, will venture to judge a brother who fails to stand fast by the faith in this or in any other respect. But it remains true that if the Christian way is, as we believe, God's way for the world, then it is only by fidelity to that way that men can ever expect the endorsement of Heaven. Until, therefore, the church refuses to sanction the methods of the battlefield under any circumstances or for any purpose, however lofty or plausible, she can never speak with a voice that will command either the approval of God or the response of men. The church professes that the gospel of Jesus Christ can solve every problem which arises from the clash of good and evil: the gospel is thus God's " good news " to a sinful world. But obviously, if in time of crisis that gospel must give way to the brutality of armed conflict, then it is not " good news " but merely a "sounding gong and a clanging cymbal." Why should the world listen to the church in regard to other issues when, in regard to this supreme issue, she speaks with an uncertain voice and in hesitating and even conflicting accents?

The nineteenth century saw the end of chattel-slavery in the civilized world because the conscience of Christian men condemned it; and the same may be true in the twentieth century in this matter of international war. But all depends upon the church and her fidelity to the authority of Christ. Meantime, the world is burdened by its weight of armaments, and civilization lives under the constant threat of destruction, just because the church is hesitant and uncertain. Only one thing will avail: the Christian passion which led a David Livingstone to war against the slave trade must inspire all Christian people to war against war. No prayer, therefore, can befit us better in that crusade than the dying words of Livingstone himself, now inscribed upon his tomb in Westminster Abbey: "May Heaven's rich blessing come down on everyone — American, English, Turk — who will help to heal this open sore of the world."

PART II

POLITICAL: THE CHRISTIAN'S
CONTRIBUTION TO PEACE

CHAPTER VIII

THE POSITIVE APPROACH TO THE PROBLEM

IN A brilliant exposure of what he calls the " war convention," Mr. A. A. Milne opens his case in the following terms: " The Prime Minister and Sir John Simon think that modern war is disastrous; I think that war is wrong. The Pope and the Archbishop of Canterbury think that modern war is horrible; I think that war is wrong. Lord Beaverbrook and Lord Rothermere think that modern war puts too great a burden on the taxpayer: I think that war is wrong." [1]

Nevertheless the Christian case is reinforced if it can be shown that what is wrong is also inexpedient; for Christian people and good citizens of all kinds are induced to support warlike methods in certain emergencies, because they believe that benefits can be secured by the successful use of armed force which, in the final balance, will outweigh the losses and the ills which war itself inflicts.

It would require a skilled review of every war in history, and an unbiased assessment of the complex results of each, to demonstrate the truth or falsity of this be-

---

[1] *Peace with Honor*, by A. A. Milne (Methuen & Company, London), p. 8.

lief; but — in the light of the Christian faith — it is
reasonable to hold that any method of achieving spiritual or moral ends which conflicts with the will and
way of God, as seen in Jesus Christ, is bound in the long
run to miscarry. This is not to say that armed force is
incapable of achieving results of a certain kind: [2] it can
for instance and it has on occasion imposed the will of
one people upon another or prevented such imposition.
As a brilliant historical student has told us: "War in
history is a real and important factor: it has settled certain things: it made (ancient) Britain a united England: it made the dominant European influence in
India English and not French . . . it turned back the
flood tide of Turkish conquest from the gates of Vienna
in 1683." [3]   So also the attempt of the Spanish crown
to impose Roman Catholicism upon England and the
Low Countries was defeated by war: the American
Colonies won their political independence by an appeal to arms; and similarly down the years.

But while it cannot be questioned that war again and

[2] Mr. John Buchan, in discussing the Cromwellian settlement in Ireland, says: "It was a dogma of the elder liberalism that violence can never
achieve anything, and that persecution so far from killing a thing must
inevitably nourish it. For such optimism there is no warrant in history:
time and again violence has achieved its purpose." (*Oliver Cromwell*, by
John Buchan, p. 355.) From the Christian point of view, everything
depends upon the kind of reaction which the persecuted make to the
operations of violence: it was, for example, the specific reaction of Jesus to
his murderers — and not the mere fact of his death — which made his
crucifixion an ultimate triumph instead of a final disaster.

[3] *The Place of War in History*, an address by Bernard L. Manning to
the Assembly of the Congregational Union of England and Wales, October
9, 1929.

again has altered the course of history, there are limits to what can be achieved by physical violence; and those limits are frequently disregarded when the efficacy of armed force is stressed. These limits will be referred to in a subsequent chapter, and the political alternatives to war will be duly considered: but it will clear the ground if at the outset we emphasize war's ineffectiveness in certain directions; for the illusion of its all-round efficacy is deeply ingrained in human tradition, and for that reason is difficult to dislodge. Two or three familiar instances may be cited by way of illustration.

It is, for example, almost axiomatic in England, especially among Nonconformists, to ascribe the establishment of civil and religious liberty to the strong arm of Oliver Cromwell, the Lord Protector of the Realm from 1653 to 1658. The position is generally accepted without question. By a series of brilliant military victories, Cromwell overthrew the absolute monarchy of Charles I and dislodged prelacy from its position of power: the principle of a " free church in a free state " seemed to have triumphed; and in many a chapel vestry today, throughout the length and breadth of England, a portrait of Cromwell adorns the walls in token of that alleged fact. But it is none the less a gross misreading of history. For Cromwell was hardly gone to his grave (from which he was disinterred by his former enemies a few years later) when Charles II and his ministers placed vindictive legislation upon the Statute Book, penalizing, imprisoning, and deporting the Nonconformists for asserting the liberties which Cromwell had fought to secure. The Corporation Act, the Act of Uniformity, the Conventicle Act and the Five Mile Act were all passed within less than a decade of Cromwell's death; and they were the means of destroying every shred of freedom which Nonconformists owed to the violent methods of the Lord Protector: thousands suffered the deprivation of their rights, their property, their position. The simple-minded Pepys, whose *Diary* throws light on the social conditions of the time, met some of the Nonconformists on their way to jail. " They go like lambs," he writes, " without any resistance: I would to God they would conform, or be more wise and not be catched "! Gardiner, the historian, commenting on these events, says: " It was fear which produced the eagerness of English gentlemen to persecute Dissenters. They remembered how they themselves had been kept under by Cromwell's Puritan army, and knowing that most of Cromwell's soldiers were still in the prime of life, they feared lest if the Dissenters were allowed to gather head, they might become strong enough to call again to arms that ever-victorious army." [4] As always, persecution overreached itself and provoked a reaction: yet it took nearly thirty years of quiet heroism on the part of the persecuted to secure the remission of the penal legislation; for it was not until 1689 that the Toleration Act gave to Nonconformists the constitutional right to exercise liberty in regard to public worship. It was not militarism but martyrdom which won the day; and the Nonconform-

[4] *A Student's History of England*, by S. R. Gardiner, p. 588.

ists gained by suffering in the name of Christ what they failed to achieve by the sword of Cromwell.

The story of the Scottish Covenanters points the same moral. On the field of battle — at Rullion Green and Bothwell Brig — they were routed, and tyranny triumphed. By 1680 the Covenanters were defeated and their power of military resistance was broken. But though they could no longer kill for their faith, brave men and women still dared to die for it: and in eight short years they won on the scaffold and at the stake the liberties which they invariably lost on the field of battle. As in the early centuries, it was " the blood of the martyrs " — and not of the soldiers — which was " the seed of the church " and the substance of Christian liberty.

Another illustration may be found in the history of modern Italy. Liberal-minded people bestow their acclamations upon Garibaldi and his thousand men as the liberators of that country; and nothing can ever dim the heroism of that splendid struggle. But the place of Garibaldi in the Temple of Fame is not rightly seized until we see it in relation to the figure of Mussolini, whose proud boast it is to have " trampled upon the corpse of liberty." For Mussolini has merely captured and exploited that same principle of violence which Garibaldi exalted and perpetuated when he drew the sword to expel the Bourbons. Liberty was the goal and aim of Garibaldi's violence, as it was with Oliver Cromwell, but Liberty and Violence are an ill-assorted pair, and a marriage between them always suffers final dissolution through incompatibility of temperament.

Abraham Lincoln is another name frequently quoted when the legitimacy or efficacy of war for some great end is questioned. Did not Lincoln free the American slaves by force of arms? Even John Bright — good Quaker that he was — blessed the President's military policy.[5] But was there no other way, and has the military way issued in the freedom for which men fought and died? Chattel-slavery, as a legalized institution in the southern states, was abolished by the armies of the North; but if the liberty of the Negro means a recognition of his human rights and respect for his personality as a child of God and a brother man, it is gravely open to question whether the American Civil War achieved anything at all for the black race in this respect. Every thoughtful American citizen today will admit that the relations between white and black constitute one of the most stubborn problems that the United States has to face; and it is not unusual to hear Negroes declare that if war was necessary to liberate the black from legal bondage, it may be necessary again in order to ensure freedom from social oppression and the denial of elementary human rights by the dominant white race. Whatever else it did, the Civil War certainly did not solve the problem of interracial relations: on the contrary it tended to embitter them, for the

---

[5] See Bright's letter to Villiers, August 5, 1863: "I want no end of the war, and no compromise, and no reunion till the Negro is made free beyond all chance of failure."

Negroes naturally sided with the enemies of the southerners: and there are many who hold that there was more essential liberty for the Negro in the slave-plantation days than there is in these days of "Jim Crow cars" and anti-Negro legislation and not infrequent lynchings.

Be that as it may, it is by no means necessary to accept the Civil War as the one and only possible means of achieving the liberation of the slaves. A few years ago a book was published [6] in which the authoress, a southern white, says: "Had the South been let alone and trusted, it would have required but a few more years for the unnatural system of human bondage to have died of itself a natural death, for it was no longer profitable." Figures indeed have been produced which show that in 1860 the capital value of a slave was greater than the capitalized wage of a free laborer. But that another way was open to the abolition of slavery — had there been the requisite Christian patience — is obvious when we recollect that in 1808 the Congress of the United States, in response to antislavery sentiment, forbade the further importation of African slaves, and that, between the founding of the American Republic and 1804, every one of the northern states had abolished slavery within its own borders. The impulse behind this action was a Christian one; and Prof. G. M. Trevelyan puts his finger on its hidden spring when he says: "The Quakers, taught by John Woolman, had

---

[6] *Southern Thoughts for Northern Thinkers,* by Mrs. Murphy, Bandanna Publishing Company, New York.

set on foot a movement toward manumission, *and no violent passion had been aroused on the opposite side."* [7] Without John Woolman, therefore, there would have been no "North" for Abraham Lincoln to lead into battle against the "South." But the tragedy of the Civil War lay in the fact that Woolman's technique and the inevitable march of economic pressure were abandoned for the short cut of military operations. An old Negro put the issue succinctly when he said: "Yes sah; there was good men on both sides, but because they couldn't think it out they had to fight it out." But violence is never an adequate substitution for thought — and still less for the Christian spirit — and America therefore still continues to pay in terms of racial strife for the failure to exercise Christian statecraft in dealing with a major social evil. In regard to the Bulgarian massacres in the 1870's, Benjamin Disraeli declared that "force is no remedy"; and the Christian who views the problem of slavery from the standpoint of essential human rights and wrongs may legitimately pass a similar verdict upon the American Civil War.

The World War of 1914–18 underlines the truth of Disraeli's dictum with startling emphasis. It was a "war to end war"; it was, in President Woodrow Wilson's words, a war "to make the world safe for democracy": according to Mr. Lloyd George, it was to make England "a land fit for heroes to dwell in." As this book is being written, it is over twenty years

[7] *The Life of John Bright,* by G. M. Trevelyan, Constable & Company, London, p. 297. Italics not in the original.

since the war started; and the high and pious aims of wartime statesmen sound today like tragic irony. The " war to end war " has led to the feverish rearmament of every nation in preparation for a " next war," infinitely more dreadful than the last: democracy, which was to be saved by force of arms, is dead and buried throughout most of Europe; even in its English birthplace it is threatened by would-be assassins masquerading in shirts of various colors: and England — like every other land in this post-war world — rewards her " heroes " by putting them on the list of the unemployed.

In view of these and countless similar facts, it is obvious that from the point of view of worldly efficacy, the case for war is frequently overstated; while from the point of view of Christian principle, as already indicated, it has no case at all. For there is no contradiction in recognizing that Cromwell and Garibaldi and Lincoln and others wrought mighty works, and yet believing that by a more fully Christian reaction to the ills they fought their work would have been even mightier.

The whole of the Christian's duty in regard to war, however, is not comprehended in a negative which refuses to make terms with armed conflict; for, by the gospel which the church professes and proclaims, Christian people are called not only to condemn the way of war, but also to organize human relationships after the pattern of a Christian fellowship. This position is implicit throughout the New Testament, and is explicitly ordained in the great law of love to God and to man, which Jesus accepted as the basis of his ethical teaching. But the law of love is not just a pretty sentiment which prohibits the bestiality and immorality of war; it is, in the Christian view, a positive energy which makes for fellowship and co-operation. For love cannot be exercised in isolation: it postulates an "other" whom we can love; or, in other words, love can only be exercised and expressed in the context of human relationships, whether those relationships are between individuals, in the family, within the nation, in the conduct of industry, or on the wider stage of world affairs.

On the positive side, therefore, the Christian's contribution to world peace is the problem of translating Christ's law of love into the policies and the political activities which govern international relationships. Briefly, the task of the Christian in this respect is to Christianize statecraft. A wartime general indicated the same task when he said, in commenting upon the vindictive clauses of the Treaty of Versailles: "Unless we will make state policy private morality writ large, there is no hope for the civilization in which we live." But this is not an easy thing to do, nor is it a matter which belongs to statesmen only and is no concern of the private citizen. Whether in a democracy or under a dictatorship that intangible, indefinable thing which we call public opinion is the finally determining factor in all matters of state policy: even a dictator cannot govern in the long run in defiance of the mass feelings and the mass convictions in whose name he acts; and

the Christian's line of approach, therefore, to the problems of international relationship and world peace must
be through a change in public opinion rather than in
the first instance through any direct influence upon
statecraft as such. How such a change in a Christian
direction can be secured will be dealt with in a subsequent chapter. But before such a change can even be
envisaged, we must first examine the conditions which
underlie international relations in the world of today,
understand some of the factors which make for war or
the fear of war, and consider the price which the Christian and his fellow citizens must be prepared to pay if
they would make an adequate contribution to world
peace.

CHAPTER IX

THE ENEMY OF WORLD PEACE

A FAMOUS British admiral who played a dramatic part in the World War recently declared that " the British navy is as safe as the Bank of England." In view of the fluctuations in the currency and the depreciation of sterling in recent years, the admiral's boast is hardly reassuring to " blue water patriots "; but he relieved their apprehensions when he went on to say that the navy " can still blast to hell anyone who opposes it," and that " none but fools believe in disarmament." On this showing, however, the army of fools would appear to be largely on the increase, for a growing number of people are turning pacifist and are coming to believe that armaments are a standing menace to the peace of the world, and even to that national security which they are supposed to guard.

The reasons for this pacifism, and the impulses which produce it, are not understood by people nurtured in the traditions of the fighting services; and many others share their misunderstanding. A pamphlet, for instance, was published a few years ago which contained a vitriolic attack upon pacifism under the caption, *The Pacifist and the Peacemaker,* and the charge was there made that pacifism encourages the temper which makes

for war rather than for peace: moreover the writer alleged that the pacifist is merely negative and never positive; and among his other vices are self-righteousness, an
undue mildness in the presence of flagrant wrong, and a
refusal to co-operate for world peace with those who
do not see eye to eye with him in every particular.
There are, of course, pacifists and pacifists, and some
may be guilty of all the charges, and more, which the
pamphleteer flings in their face. But it is strange for a
critic to complain that the pacifist is at once too mild
and too vehement: the criticisms seem to cancel each
other out. Of the two charges pacifists would probably
prefer to plead guilty to the latter rather than to the
former; but having admitted the charge they would
be inclined to deny the guilt; for we must say of a love
of truth what has been said of virtue, that if it is not
passionate it is not safe. In that sense, the vehemence
of the pacifist is a thing to rejoice over, not to lament.
There is indeed nothing more unpleasing than the
" nonresistance " which proceeds from moral indifference; and certainly the forces which jeopardize world
peace will never be met and overcome except by a burning conviction on the part of those who work and plead
for peace.

Here, as elsewhere, for the Christian the standard
is set by Jesus Christ; and it is not without significance
that he is acclaimed as at once the " Prince of Peace "
and the " Captain of our Salvation ": He was " meek " in
the presence of aggressive wrong, but he was never
merely " mild "; for mildness is not the quality which

gives good for evil and wins strong men from their enmity into eager devotion. The problem for the pacifist, however, is how to translate his convictions into practical politics. It need hardly be said that any Christian man will co-operate with others as far as he possibly can; but what does this mean in practice? how is it to be applied to foreign policy or to the idea of making the Covenant of the League of Nations effective by means of armed sanctions? This book is written in the conviction that the other side of a refusal to go to war is an endeavor to organize the world in the interests of peace. It is not enough, therefore, for the pacifist to renounce fighting as a denial of his Christian faith: this may be — and in the judgment of many it is — a necessary preliminary to any constructive effort: but if the Christian is to find an alternative to war which is also a contribution to peace, he must bring his Christian principles and his Christian citizenship to bear upon the international situation as it exists today.

That situation is one of continually changing complication, and it is generally impossible at any given moment, especially in the light of meager and often biased newspaper reports, to unravel the tangle of conflicting interests and claims which make international politics what they are. But fortunately it is not necessary to grasp every detail of every situation in order to appreciate the general character of all such situations; for there is one dominant factor which in the modern world governs the issues of war and peace, wherever and however they may be raised; and the name of that dominant factor is nationalism. Gambetta, in a famous dictum, indicated " clericalism " as the prime foe of the human race: but if he had lived in the twentieth century he would have had to revise his judgment and say, " Nationalisme, c'est l'ennemi! "

Nationalism has been described as " Man's other Religion " ; [1] and it has been pointed out [2] that " in the case of millions of people, nationalism is the only impulse which seems to have any vitality, any power to inspire and command. In Italy and in Germany nationalism is something more than a political or an economic movement: it has become a religion. Its symbols, its rituals, its anthems, its mass celebrations, its worship of the founder, its power to stir the emotions, to evoke feelings of reverence and awe — all are unmistakable characteristics of religion."

Other factors than nationalism may and do count in precipitating the crises which lead to war or the threat of war or preparation for war: but underlying or superimposed upon every such factor there is always to be found that complex of emotion and loyalty and tradition which we know as the spirit of nationalism; and apart from that spirit, though there might and would be grave problems and difficulties to be solved in the sphere of international relations, these alone would never issue in the catastrophe of war. It is therefore upon the factor of nationalism that we must concen-

[1] *Nationalism*, by Edward Shillito, Willett, Clark & Company.

[2] Article on " Christianity and Nationalism" by Ernest Fremont Tittle in *Religion and Life*, April 1934, a quarterly review published in New York.

trate our chief attention if we would discover the Christian's contribution to peace.

This point may be emphasized by a personal recollection. The writer of this book (who is English by birth) first came against nationalism as an antagonistic element at about the age of ten, when he was put to school at Grand Rapids in the State of Michigan, where his parents had settled in the late 1880's. The Middle West in those days was not far removed from the "frontier," and educational standards and methods were apt to be crude: the catechetical system was still in vogue, and history was imparted by a series of questions and answers. Most of these have dropped through the sieve of memory and there is no written record of them; but a few of them were caught on the strands of patriotic pride or resentment, and they stand out clearly to this day. The lesson started with a vivid description of the wicked " red coats " who tried to hold free citizens in chains, the " embattled farmers " who " fired the shot heard round the world," [3] the ride of Paul Revere, Washington at Valley Forge and the surrender of Cornwallis; and then came the catechism:

Question: Which was the greatest nation in the world in 1776?
Answer: The British.
Question: Why?
Answer: Because they had conquered most of the world, including the thirteen American colonies.

[3] R. W. Emerson's description in his "Hymn at the Battle Monument."

Question: Which is the greatest nation on the face of the earth today?
Answer: The United States of America.
Question: Why?
Answer: Because we beat the British! [4]

Edmund Burke's spirited defense of the colonists from his place in the House of Commons, the fact that the British government could not induce Englishmen to enlist in the fight against colonial independence, and that George III had to depend for the defense of his empire upon hired Hessians — these things were never mentioned. History was presented from first to last in terms of American nationalism. It seemed incomprehensible to one who was British-born that anyone had ever had the presumption to " beat the British "; for in England, like most boys of his age, he had acquired the idea (again mainly from the teaching of history, which in those days ended with the glories of Waterloo!) that " one Englishman was equal to three Frenchmen." The ratio of British superiority to Americans, however, had been inadvertently omitted from the curriculum; and it was therefore with sadly damaged national pride that he committed the catechism to memory.

The United States — like most other countries — has revised its history books since those far-off days; but the generation nurtured on that catechism still

[4] " We " in this case included the sons and daughters of Germans, Dutch, Scandinavian, Italian and English; only a small proportion were children of native-born Americans, and probably not one could trace American ancestry as far back as the War of Independence.

votes nationalist senators into Congress, and still believes that the country's greatness turns upon the ability
to " beat the British " or any other breed of foreigners
who may cross the path of national ambition.

It is this virus of nationalism, however induced,
which, the world over, is the enemy of world peace
and the standing obstacle to international understanding; and the Christian citizen therefore will make his
contribution to peace only as he takes this fact into
account. For over against the nationalisms which embitter and divide must be set a devotion which unites
all men for the common good. The Christian ideal in
this respect is set forth in the vision of the Seer (in the
Book of the Revelation) when he declares that " the
kingdoms of the world are become the empire of our
Lord and his Christ," and it is to the achievement of
that goal that the Christian citizen must bend his
energies.

What this means in terms of existing political reality
is the theme with which this book is concerned. If
nationalism is a religion, it can only be met by a religious
impulse which is more potent than the worship of the
state; and if the tribal and national gods which today
claim and win men's devotion are to be dethroned, it
can only be by the enthronement of a God whose claims
are greater than the claims of any earthly state, and
whose power to win the hearts of men transfers to himself the service which is now given with such lavish
abandon to " the kingdoms of the world and the glory
of them."

CHAPTER X

THE MEANING OF NATIONALISM

It is axiomatic to say that international relations play an increasing part in the world's life, whether in war or in peace. This fact is often thought to be the concern only of statesmen; but it lies behind the simplest and commonest events of everyday experience; for the ordinary life of the ordinary citizen is what it is by reason of the fact that economically — through the processes of international trade — he can reach to the ends of the earth for the satisfaction of his simplest wants. The whole world contributes daily to his comfort and convenience in material things. What is true of material things is also true of things of the mind and the spirit; for art, literature, song, architecture, education, religion, are the creation of no single nation, but a gift to humanity contributed by all mankind in the successive ages of the world's history. The fact, indeed, is so obvious as to make detailed illustration superfluous.

This ability, however, to levy toll on the world at large depends upon the maintenance of international peace; for a state of war immediately isolates nations one from the other, and under the existing economic order depresses the standard of living. Those who remember the rationing of food and other commodities during the World War will need no convincing on this point; for even the control of the seas by the Allied Powers did little more than allow the bare necessities of existence to enter the embattled countries. Among the Central Powers and in countries far removed from the seaboard, this disastrous lowering of the standard of living had effects upon the population which will not be outlived for at least a generation; the restricted war diet upon which the European countries were compelled to subsist is estimated to have resulted in the death through famine of over a million Serbian and Austrian civilians. It was reported early in 1919, by relief agencies operating in Poland, that no Polish child under six had survived the war-starvation of 1914–18; in Russia figures were notoriously inaccurate, but conservative estimates give a figure of two million as the number of those who perished through the privations imposed by four years of fighting and subsequent civil war; tuberculosis among German children between the ages of five and fifteen increased by 75 per cent between 1913 and 1920; and similar figures could be adduced almost indefinitely.

There is also another way in which war depresses the standard of living; for the money which is wasted in the prosecution of hostilities leaves — again under the existing economic system — a colossal burden of debt which prevents social progress and reconstruction in post-war years. A few figures relating to British expenditure will make this clear. In 1914 the cost of the war to the British taxpayer was $5,000,000 a day; in 1918 this figure had risen to $35,000,000, and even today three-quarters of British taxation is spent upon paying for past wars or preparing for future wars; the cost of maintaining armaments in anticipation of a war which nobody desires is no less than $1000 a minute, year in and year out. It is no wonder, therefore, that social services are crabbed, education starved, and the wheel of social progress everywhere retarded. The construction of a modern battleship (which is obsolescent by the time it is built) costs $35,000,000, for which figure no less than 20,000 new houses could be built; it has been computed that the same figure would build 50 hospitals, lay 50 miles of arterial roads, 100 miles of country roads, provide 100 recreation grounds, erect 100 schools, and completely furnish 4000 working-class dwellings. The annual maintenance of a battleship is $3,000,000, or the equivalent of 1500 houses a year. The cost of firing a single round from a 16-inch gun is $10,500, for which sum it would be possible to give old-age pensions for one week to 4200 people. The preliminary British bombardment, during the war, of Arras, Messines and Passchendael cost $260,000,000, which is enough to give a million unemployed people $5 a week for an entire year. The ingenious and those interested in statistics could multiply such contrasts without limit; but the few figures quoted demonstrate conclusively that war and preparation for war cannot coexist with a high standard of living or with an adequate recognition of social responsibility. It follows, therefore, that the maintenance of peace and of friendly international relations is among the most important questions with which the citizen can be concerned. Yet in spite of this fact, all nations prepare elaborate and costly armaments for a war which no one desires but which every nation fears may be thrust upon it by the aggression or attack of some neighbor nation.

The question, therefore, comes to every mind which ponders the situation: Why is the nation the only group or association which lives in constant fear of attack and arms against it? No other organized group is obsessed by this fear; the churches, trade unions, Rotary clubs, literary and scientific societies, athletic associations, political parties, and all such organizations live together in these days with no thought of " defense "; and in many cases they are international in character, so that they are unable to claim the protection of national armies and navies to ensure their continued existence. Then is there anything in the quality or character of a nation which makes it different from these other human associations? And if so, what?

Many answers have been given and certain elements have been indicated as indispensable to nationhood. Any map shows the several nations occupying a definite territory; but many other associations are also organized territorially, and we must therefore find other characteristics than those of territorial integrity as the distinguishing mark of nationality. There are several factors which are thought to differentiate a nation from other human groupings. The most obvious of these is a natural frontier; that is, people within certain geographical limits are regarded as constituting a nation.

But the political structure of the world reveals the inadequacy of this suggestion. Canada and the United States of America, for instance, are both of them nations in the ordinary sense of that word, yet the frontiers which divide them are for the most part conventional; the Austrian South Tyrol is now included in the kingdom of Italy, despite the natural frontier which existed in pre-war days and which was moved after the war for strategic reasons. Poland is notoriously a country with no natural frontier on the east, yet no one would deny that the Polish people have a strong sense of nationality. The fact is that frontiers are movable features, and as such they cannot be accounted as an indubitable mark of nationhood.

The modern German ideal suggests a common racial origin as the differentia of a nation; but Germany's western neighbor makes this theory untenable; for Belgium, like many other nations in the modern world, has a conflict of races within her national boundaries; and indeed the struggle between Flemings and Walloons is one of the acute domestic problems with which Belgian statesmanship is frequently called to deal. Great Britain traces its ancestry as a nation to races so diverse as Celts and Saxons and Normans, while the United States of America, with its notorious intermixture of races from all over the globe, is for that reason frequently known as " the melting pot."

A common language is sometimes cited as the defining factor; but nations like Switzerland, India, South Africa or Canada (to mention only a few) are bilingual or multilingual, and yet to none of them could we deny the name of nation.

The same objection holds when a common government is held to constitute a nation. Pre-dominion Ireland and the pre-war Austrian Empire had each of them a common government, and yet the power to govern broke upon the fact of conflicting nationalisms within the same territory.

It is the fashion nowadays to find the explanation of most things in terms of economic interest, and it is of course true that each nation possesses its own currency, erects its own tariffs, promulgates its own industrial legislation, and is in general responsible for the economic relationships of its people. But it is increasingly apparent that both labor and capital have more community of interest with similar groups in other nations than with opposite groups within the same nation; indeed the *bête-noire* of organized labor in these days is "international capital," which transcends national groupings, and vice versa. It is not without significance that it was in the name of nationalism that the German Reich suppressed the trade unions with their international affiliations.

None of these answers, therefore, is adequate to explain the existence of nationhood; frontiers, race, language, government, economic interests — all these are doubtless associated in greater or less degree with national life, but in and of themselves they do not explain it. For the essence of nationality, that which binds people into a nation, is something more impalpable than any outward or material bond, and it can only be defined as a common spirit. It is this common spirit animating a people who dwell within a common frontier and accept a common government which makes a nation a separate entity and distinguishes it from others. This fact was expressed in a curious episode shortly after the conclusion of the American Civil War in 1865. The Triennial Convention of the Protestant Episcopal church in those days proposed a new form of prayer which began with the petition: "O God, the only Lord and Ruler of all the peoples upon earth, bless this our nation." The American Republic, however, had too recently been torn by internal strife to allow the regrowth of that common spirit which made it one at the time of the Declaration of Independence; there was a common frontier, to a large extent a common race (for the British element was dominant), a common language, a common government, and to a limited degree common economic interests; but without the imponderable element of a common ideal and a common spirit, the nation existed only in form and not in reality. Consequently the proposed petition was amended by the convention, and it still stands in the church's Prayer Book in these terms: "O God, the only Lord and Ruler of all the peoples upon earth, bless these United States." In other words, at that time the spiritual unity of the several states was felt to be too loose to justify the word "nation."

This conception of nationality as a common life or a community of people within a common territory and

organized by a common spirit, is understood better by
illustration than by definition; and for this purpose one
of the most apt examples can be found in the Book of
Genesis, where the promise is made to Abraham that
he should become " a great nation," not by reason of
frontiers, or race, or language, or government, or economic interests, but by the loyalty of the Hebrews to a
common ideal and the realization of that ideal in a
political organization. So it is written, " The Lord
said unto Abraham, get thee out of thy country and
from thy kindred and from thy father's house, unto a
land that I (the Lord) will show thee: and I (the
Lord) will make of thee a great nation, and I (the
Lord) will bless thee and make thy name great; and
thou shalt be a blessing." [1]   Thus in the case of the
Hebrews the nation cohered about a religious ideal,
which was the dream of a God-governed people or a
theocracy.

It is not necessary, however, that the national ideal
should be of a religious character; for anything which
inspires common devotion to a common cause may be
the focus about which a nation may be organized.
Modern political philosophy stresses this fact when it
declares that a nation is a community " held together
and apart from others by the consciousness of being a
people, sharing on a common soil certain rather subtle
characteristics and qualities which require for their
expression a single political government. It depends
on no one definite attribute, such as race or language

[1] Genesis xii. 1 and 2.

or religion or custom or tradition. It has its roots in history, but history alone does not explain it. *It is the active sense of belonging together.*" [2]

Originally this "sense of belonging together" came from the impulse of self-preservation against nature or for protection against a common enemy: and in so far as this was the case, it is true to say that the first movements toward nationality were inspired by self-interest. It is this fact indeed which still accounts for the exclusive and self-sufficient elements inherent in the modern conception of a nation, and the association of nationality with the idea of military defense.

But the need for self-preservation is not the only factor which induces a "sense of belonging together." In the United States, for instance, the historic ideal of civil and religious liberty implicit in American history is one of the elements which bind the citizens together; anyone who has felt the emphasis of American elementary education in this respect cannot but be aware of the reality of this factor in the make-up of American nationality. The tradition of parliamentary government in England, with the habit of open discussion and freedom of utterance, plays a dominant part in the national life of Britain. The same is true of trivial social traits which seem to the foreign observer to be merely curiosities of national habit; the Englishman's love of cricket, the American's passion for baseball, the Italian's taste for macaroni, the German's *bier garten,* the Frenchman's café, the Russian's *samovar* — all these

[2] *Social Science,* by R. M. Maciver, p. 39. Italics not in the original.

make men feel at home in a given group, and so give that " sense of belonging together " which is of the essence of nationality. What we call " good form " may seem superficially to be a mere matter of deportment or custom, yet it may play an important part in engendering a feeling of community with our fellow citizens; the way a man uses his knife and fork at table will mark him in a foreign country either as a native or a stranger; his drawing-room etiquette declares at once his national affiliations; the Englishman's eyes gleam whenever he is offered a cup of tea in the United States, and the American in England, by a strange paradox, warms at the very thought of ice cream! It is in this way that the citizens of a nation are bound together by a multitude of subtle and indefinable links, alike historical, sentimental, practical, emotional, cultural, economic and religious; and it is when people, thus bound together by spiritual community, are organized within a certain territory by common laws and common institutions and common government that collectively they are described as a " nation." The word " state " is then used to designate the nation when it is organized politically, and when through the power of government, it exercises authority or sovereignty over the lives of its citizens.

This definition of a nation-state is important because it enables us to understand what are the legitimate demands of the state upon the citizen, and what are the principles which may rightly govern international or interstate relations. Certain facts, therefore, must be taken into account if we would give the state its legitimate place in human life.

The philosophical conception of the state was first formulated by the Greeks; and their conception was necessarily determined by their particular political experience, which was limited by the confines of the city-state as it then existed. To Plato and Aristotle, for instance, the entire life of the citizen was comprehended in and provided for by the state: through its medium — and through it alone — he found his religion, his art, his education, his music, his liberty, his justice, his all. The " politics " of Aristotle include the playing of the flute, and with Plato poetry is a department of the state's activities. But today the city-state (with its all-inclusive economy) has gone, and the modern citizen finds the satisfactions which make life worth living and give it amplitude and value, not only through the activities of the state as such, but also through a variety of groups and *ad hoc* communities, which as often as not transcend the territorial limits of the state. This is true of churches and missionary societies, commercial and financial companies, cultural movements of all kinds, philanthropic organizations such as the anti-slavery movement, quarantine and health regulations, aviation (which of necessity ignores frontiers), the radio (which brings both speech and music from the ends of the earth to the humblest citizen's receiving set), political institutions like the League of Nations or the Inter-Parliamentary Union, and so on. Consequently the state in the modern world is but one community among a multitude of others, and its prime function, philosophically considered, is not to dominate the life of the citizen, but to guarantee his access to all the means of culture which are offered by the modern world.

It follows from this that the nation-state is not in any sense sacrosanct, nor is it endowed with any super-moral authority which gives it a right to ride roughshod over the meanest of its citizens. The state is endowed with coercive force — through its police and judiciary — only in order that it may prevent the coercion of one citizen or group of citizens by another, and so ensure — in an atmosphere of freedom — the mutual well-being of the several communities in and through which the citizens find fulness of life.

All this means that the philosophical idea of the state, as formulated by Greek thinkers, is no longer adequate: for no such institution as the Greek city-state now exists. So long as the citizen's entire life was comprehended within the limits of the state (as was the case under the Greek economy) the defense of the state could legitimately be regarded as the citizen's prime duty. But today — when man's life is fulfilled in numberless associations, many of which are wider than the state itself — the defense of the state by force of arms is no longer the sole desideratum. For to embark upon military defense is to cut off and even destroy many of those wider groupings whose maintenance ministers to human life as greatly as, and in some respects much more than, the maintenance of the state. From the point of view of political philosophy, therefore, the duty of defending the state is no longer paramount; for it is as important to preserve those cultural and other associations which contribute to the widest life of the citizen (but which are always menaced by war) as to maintain that political association which we call the state.[3] In other words, the nation-state is no more worthy of defense than are the international affiliations which give to human life its fulness and its variety; and consequently the main task of the citizen is to forswear the operations of war and to maintain at all costs a peaceful international order, under which alone the varied and various groups by which human life is fulfilled can flourish. It is a realization of this fact which has led so many of the youth in the universities of Britain and America and the dominions to declare their refusal ever to " fight for King and Country," or — as in the United States — to " fight for Flag and Country." [4]

What seems to have happened in the international realm is that the facts of political life have outrun the common man's philosophic interpretation of them; so that today current political ideas of the sovereign state are derived from outworn Greek conceptions which, though adequate as an interpretation of the Greek city-

[3] The modern totalitarian state, by discounting international affiliations, impoverishes the life of its citizens and sets itself in opposition to the fact of world interdependence: it cannot therefore be a permanent feature of political life, for the whole trend of world events is against it.

[4] All but two of the British universities have, in various student societies, passed antiwar resolutions in recent years; while in the United States no less than seventy colleges have gone on record to a similar effect.

state, are no longer capable of expressing the realities of modern political life. It is these outworn conceptions which still govern the political traditions of the masses, and even the thinking and action of statesmen, and so cause nation-states the world over to regard defense by preparation for war as the chief duty of the citizen. What is true of the Greek political philosophy is no less true of all those philosophies which isolate the state as a self-sufficient and sovereign entity; Machiavelli and Hobbes and Hegel are in this respect as much out of date as Aristotle; for they conceive of contacts with other states in terms mainly of conflict. The outstanding feature of modern international life, however — as already indicated — is that contact between states is in terms of co-operation and interdependence rather than of strife; and every true philosophy of the modern state therefore sees it as an organization for bringing national groups into association, in spite of local and natural differences, in order that each nationality may make its specific contribution to the culture and well-being of all mankind. Moreover, this international association is not occasional — as in the ancient world of isolated communities — but continuous and world-wide.[5] In this way the very pressure of circumstance is endorsing the Christian ideal of world fellowship; and in such a world, war is an anachronism and as much a violation of national self-interest as it is of the Christian spirit and the Christian ideal.

[5] For an elaboration of this point of view see *Community*, by R. Maciver.

In view of this conception of the state it is possible to appreciate a distinction which is often ignored in thinking or speaking of international affairs; and that is the distinction between national*ism* and national*ity*. Nationality is nothing other than the " sense of belonging together " in an organized political community, and as such one nationality can coexist with any number of others in intimate contact and co-operation. This of course is the fact upon which the League of Nations is founded. But national*ism* bears the same sinister relation to national*ity* as does individual*ism* to individual*ity:* every person who pulls his weight in human affairs has individuality, something which marks him off from other persons and gives him characteristics by which he is distinguished from the mass of his fellows: but when a person pursues his own interests regardless of social consequences and heedless of the good of his neighbors, then that which distinguishes him from his fellows becomes the enemy of the common weal, and the blessing of individual*ity* becomes the curse of individual*ism*. It is the same with the nation. To conserve national characteristics is to cherish something without which the whole human family would be poorer; but to claim for any nation the right to do as it will among the community of nations, to assert the superiority of a given national group over other such groups, to proclaim national " sovereignty " as the final warrant of state action — that is of the essence of national*ism,* and it is as destructive of human well-being in the international sphere as individualism is in the social sphere. It is plain, therefore, to everyone who contemplates the armed and rival nationalisms of today, that only as this menace is held in check can humanity avoid the catastrophe of a disastrous world war, which will destroy the gains of the centuries and leave behind only the so-called peace of the desert. "Nationalisme, c'est l'ennemi!"

CHAPTER XI

NATIONALISM AND ECONOMICS

NATIONALISM (which is an amalgam of tribal instincts
and traditions and historic memories and sentimental
attachments and unthinking loyalties) is the real enemy of world peace; and the Christian's contribution to
peace, therefore, must reckon with that fact if it is to
operate in the realm of political reality.

This thesis, however, is strongly and often violently
challenged by people who — consciously or uncon-
sciously — follow Karl Marx in finding the explanation of all things in the domain of economics. From
this point of view international tensions and rivalries
are all of them accounted for by certain obvious or hidden economic antagonisms; in particular the prevailing
order of capitalism is held to be responsible, since, impelled by the profit-making motive or by what Mr.
R. H. Tawney calls " the incentive of private gain," [1]
its prime requisite under an economy of large-scale
machine production is markets; and it is in the endeavor to secure or to monopolize these markets that
nations threaten or engage in war. Then — by a process which the logician would describe as *non sequitur*
— the conclusion is drawn that the only basis of world

[1] *The Acquisitive Society*, by R. H. Tawney, passim.

peace is the destruction of capitalism and the erection
of a socialistic order in its place.

It is not within the scope of this book to discuss the
merits or the demerits of socialist economics, except to
say in passing that every Christian must have a lively
sympathy with the endeavor to substitute for the competitive game of beggar-my-neighbor in the economic
world an order of life upon a co-operative basis governed by intelligent planning. This process of substitution will begin — as indeed it is beginning — by the
reconstruction of the economic ordering of each several
nation within its own borders; but the Christian ideal
no less than practical necessity points to the creation of
a co-operative world order as the final goal. It is obvious, therefore, that war must be outlawed if the common ordering of the world's economic life is ever to be
achieved and maintained. But precisely for this reason
the problem of war and peace is of primary importance;
for unless we can rid civilization of the menace of war
the dream of a co-operative order is forever impossible.
Then can we abolish war without first abolishing capitalism? Is international peace possible in a capitalist
world? If not, the omens seem to indicate that war is
likely to occur long before a new social order is established, and in that case — as will be indicated later —
the task of the social idealist would be not to transform
capitalism into co-operation, but to start afresh at the
very bottom by organizing order out of chaos. It is
generally admitted that another war on a world scale
would throw civilization back into primitive barbarism,

and the steady and painful gains of the centuries in enhancing human well-being would be trampled in ruins. It is of the utmost importance, therefore, to determine whether war can be eliminated from human intercourse before or only after a radical reconstruction of the economic order. Present-day tendencies would seem to justify the conclusion that unless we can first get rid of war, all our social idealisms will be frustrated by the utter destruction of any semblance of an economic order. Someone has outlined the situation by saying that " war is nearer than socialism "; and therefore the prime necessity which is laid upon those who seek to order life on a Christian basis is to eliminate the possibility of war in order that — within the context of world peace — they may give themselves with undivided energy to the reconstruction of the social fabric.

That economic factors enter into international relations and are one of the elements involved in the issues of war and peace is not questioned; but an examination of the international situation, whether in days gone by or today, warrants the assertion that unless nationalistic passion be superimposed upon economic strife, the latter does not of itself issue in war.[2] But this means that nationalism and not capitalism is the prime enemy of world peace; or, in other words, political rather than

[2] We are not here considering what is called the " class-war," which is of course the direct outcome of economic struggle; the term " class-war " is really a figure of speech, for organized capital and labor as such do not arm themselves for battle against opposing forces, as nations do by the organization of armies and navies and air forces.

economic factors are the chief element in the situation. Acute economic rivalries exist throughout the world between opposing groups, but they do not explode in active warfare unless they can utilize the pretext of nationalism as a cloak for their commercial and financial ambitions. It has been alleged that American marines during the 1920's invaded Nicaragua in order to secure the dividends of the United Fruit Company; but even if this be so, not a single " doughboy " would have shouldered a rifle or marched a single step unless he had first come to believe that he was fighting, not for the United Fruit Company, but for the United States. In spite of the allegations of " dollar diplomacy," nationalism and not capitalism was the operative impulse which made the military occupation possible.

The same is true even when the economic factor takes the form of trade in armaments.[3] The faith of the armament manufacturer has been pilloried by Mr. Bernard Shaw in his *Major Barbara,* when he puts these words into the mouth of Undershaft, the munitions maker: " To give arms to all men who offer an honest

[3] For a thoroughgoing exposure of the sinister and cynical enterprise of selling implements of death for the sake of profits, the reader is referred to the following books: *The Secret International* and *Patriotism Ltd.*, both published by the Union of Democratic Control; *The Bloody Traffic,* by A. Fenner Brockway; *The Merchants of Death*, by Englebrecht and Hanighen; *Iron, Blood and Profits*, by George Seldes; or he may consult the report of investigations by a Commission of the United States Senate into the private manufacture of armaments. A popular and nontechnical account of the armaments business is contained in *Cry Havoc*, by Beverley Nichols.

price for them, without respect of persons or principles; to aristocrats and republicans, to Nihilists and Tzar, to Capitalist and Socialist, to Protestant and Catholic, to burglar and policeman, to black man, white man and yellow man, to all sorts and conditions, all nationalities, all faiths, all follies, all causes, and all crimes. . . . Government of this country? I am the Government of this country!" But, while no one who knows the facts will question the accuracy of this picture, not even Undershaft could sell a single rifle or tank or submarine or bombing plane unless he were able to play upon fear of the foreigner, and to appeal to nationalistic pride. Apart from these impulses (which at bottom are matters of psychology and not of economics), no government in the world would yield to his solicitation for orders.

This conclusion (that nationalism is the evil genius determining the issues of war and peace) is reinforced when we remember that economic interests just as often clash within the same frontier as across frontiers; yet in the former case the clash never induces " war-talk," while in the latter it only too frequently does. It is one of the commonest fallacies implicit in our common speech to regard nations as economic units which engage in foreign trade; we speak, for instance, of British trade or French trade or German trade, when what we are actually referring to is trade by British firms (whose shares may even be held by foreign investors), or French firms or German firms as the case may be. In the modern world Soviet Russia is the only instance where the identification of the nation with a trading concern is even approximately true, and in all other cases it is incorrect to assume that economic interests coincide with frontiers. Yet it is this false assumption which lies behind the plea that economic interests are primarily responsible for war.

The relevant facts lie ready to hand. For instance, Danish foodstuffs compete with the produce of English dairy farms, but — as fervent imperialists have discovered to their dismay — so do foodstuffs from the British dominions. The cotton trade of Lancashire is seriously menaced by the cotton mills of Tokio, and in consequence Japan to many people becomes the " enemy " of Great Britain and there is wild talk of increasing the British naval ratio in order to teach the Japanese a much-needed lesson; but when the cotton industry of Lanarkshire was extinguished half a century ago by the better situated and better equipped industry of Lancashire, not even the most perfervid patriot north of the Border dreamed of precipitating war between Scotland and England. The economic rivalry was there, but the poison of nationalism could not be invoked to stir it into military activity. Sir Norman Angell has pointed to a similar conflict of economic interest in the United States: " The American manufacturer in Massachusetts," he says, " will assert heatedly the need for protecting his workers against the cheap labor of Belgium or Britain; but it does not occur to him to think of protecting them against the cheap labor of South Carolina. But he would demand protection from South Carolina as a matter of course if the American colonies which are now the United States had, like the American colonies of Spain, developed into separate nations. The American manufacturer would have to deal with exactly the same men and women turning out exactly the same goods, as he does at the present moment; but if the Carolinas or Louisiana were a nation, as might so easily have been the case if the history of North America had followed the line of South America, he would talk alarmingly of the competition of Louisiana — as alarmingly as we talk of that of Belgium or Czechoslovakia or Germany." [4]

The possibility of rival nationalisms in the Carolinas and Louisiana may seem absurd to the United States citizen of today, for even in the American Civil War they were both on the same side of the conflict; yet it was little more than a series of historic accidents which prevented such a condition from becoming an accomplished fact. This is clear if we consult a map of the North American continent in 1800. What is now the United States of America, stretching from the Atlantic to the Pacific and from the Great Lakes to the Gulf of Mexico, then consisted of no less than six separate sovereignties or potential sovereignties; the original thirteen states existed as an independent republic; the existing states of Alabama and Mississippi were claimed by their Creek Indian inhabitants as a separate nation; Florida and a coastal strip westward to the Mississippi

[4] *The Unseen Assassins,* by Sir Norman Angell, p. 85.

River were under the Spanish Crown; Louisiana and
the whole of the Mississippi Valley were French; the region now extending from Texas to California was
Spanish; while the states of Oregon, Washington and
Idaho were as yet unappropriated to any sovereignty
and were vaguely claimed as part of the British colonial
dominions. Subsequent history threw all these regions
under the government of the United States; the Creek
Indians failed to substantiate their claim to separate
nationality, Florida was ceded to the United States in
1819, Napoleon Buonaparte sold the Louisiana territory
to the American Republic in 1803, the southwest region
ceased to be Spanish by 1853, and the delimitation of
the northwestern territories was amicably settled with
Great Britain in 1846. Suppose, however, that the political divisions of 1800 had been perpetuated as the
American continent was explored and developed!
There would then have been a United States seaboard,
a native Indian Alabama, a French Louisiana, a Spanish California and Florida, and a British Northwest
Territory; and it is easy to see, therefore, that the history of the United States and its present condition
would have been not greatly unlike that of Europe.
That is to say, the United States of America would not
have been a federal unity but a group of sovereign
states, each one with different laws, different customs,
a different language, different currencies, each with separate armies and navies, each protected by tariffs against
all the rest, and each possessing its own national tradition, its own patriotism, its own flag, and its own gov-

ernment. Then as a result of these rival nationalisms, economic disputes would have gathered patriotic sentiment about them, and the student of international affairs would have been told today that capitalism in North America made war inevitable.

Yet in reality the cause of those wars which have not taken place would have lain not in economic rivalry but in the spirit of nationalism; for plainly the reason why European nations arm one against the other and the states of the American Union do not, lies in the fact that the former are organized on a basis of separate sovereignty, while the latter are included in a federated society of communities. It is true that even the federal constitution of the United States did not prevent one of the bloodiest wars in history between North and South; but the breakdown of the federal structure at that particular point is no argument for the scrapping of constitutions, but only for the strengthening of them by the support of public opinion, until sectional loyalties shall no longer be capable of inducing disloyalty to the federal union. The American Civil War was associated with the economic situation created by the competition between slave labor and the wage earner; but the economic antagonism could never have been fanned into the flames of war had it not been fed by the nationalistic and separatist traditions (which still exist to an astonishing extent in the American South) carried down from the days when each state was a quasi-sovereign entity.

When we look at the alleged economic causation of

war from a human standpoint, it is obvious that armies
consist of " proletarians " as well as " capitalists," and
the economic interests of the common soldier on both
sides of a given conflict coincide to a far greater degree
than they clash; it is in the interests of the common
people everywhere to work in harmony and to exchange the products of their labor rather than to fight.
War in any case impoverishes those to whom we would
sell our goods if we could, and the story of the post-war
depression — with its commercial collapse, its repudiation of debts, its financial disintegration — ought to
dispose once and for all of the illusion that war is a
paying proposition even to capitalist interests. During
the World War certain Allied commercial interests
loudly proclaimed their patriotic intention to " capture
German trade," and " to make Germany pay." But before many years had run, Allied financial houses were
seeking to save German trade by the granting of liberal
credits, and even German reparations for wartime damage to Allied property were scaled down and finally
canceled because their payment was inflicting economic
damage upon Allied industry. The world over, war
debts have gone into liquidation, and those who sought
economic gain through victory have suffered as greatly
as, and in some cases even more so than, the van-
quished. If one thing is certain it is that war, under
modern conditions of economic interdependence, does
not pay; and if, therefore, economic profit is alleged as
the sole cause of war, the allegation rests upon a demon-
strable illusion.

Why then do the peoples of every country maintain

their armaments and from time to time engage in that
mass murder and that senseless destruction of men and
things which is the prime characteristic of modern warfare? There is only one answer, and it is found in
that compound of irrational impulses and traditional
loyalties and group antipathies and racial prejudices
which have their roots in a half-forgotten history, and
which are covered by the word "nationalism." We
therefore unduly simplify the problem of war and
peace if we regard it solely in terms of political economy; for — as stated above — unless the sentiment of
nationalism is superimposed upon economic rivalries
and antagonisms, they do not issue in international war.

There is, however, an indirect sense in which the
economic situation makes for war, and this is especially
true in times of industrial depression and widespread
unemployment. For, under the existing economic order — or disorder — the nation says in effect to great
armament firms: "So long as there is war in any part
of the world, you and your shareholders shall become
rich beyond all measure." Contrariwise, the nation says
to thousands of strong young men: "So long as there is
peace you shall stand idle in the market place, un-
wanted, your homes a desert, a meager ration of food
doled grudgingly to your family. . . . As soon as there
is war there will be work and money, you will be
needed, you will have opportunities for sacrifice and
service, and there will be a comradeship in a common
cause which shall sweeten toil and even death." [5]

[5] The contrast is quoted from an article in *No More War*, February
1934.

A few years back — as a writer on unemployment in a London weekly review has reminded us [6] — posters everywhere proclaimed " Your King and Country need you," and men in all occupations and in none, cheerfully — if somewhat blindly — responded. But today there is no poster, and the unemployed worker realizes bitterly that his king and country do not need him any longer. Little wonder, then, if in his desperation he greets his pal with the remark, " It's about time we had another bloody war! " [7]

Miss Margaret Bondfield, when she was Minister for Labor in the British Cabinet, pointed to another aspect of this connection between economics and war:

" When we talk about disarmament," she said, " and about scrapping battleships, you have to recognize the sort of pressure that will be brought to bear by trade unions and employers of labor in many parts of the country, to say nothing of the opposition from people whose money is invested in the peaceable industries involved. The more I go into this question, the more I am convinced that you cannot dissociate the problem of disarmament from the economic planning of our daily life. We have to show that we are capable of taking the large amount of money and labor that is at present misdirected to destructive purposes, and change its direction to constructive work that will promote the health, wealth and happiness of the community. Peo-

[6] *The New Statesman and Nation,* March 3, 1934.

[7] This is an exact transcript of a remark made a short time ago by a member of an occupational center for the unemployed, and it is typical of the mental outlook of multitudes.

ple do not prefer to build battleships, but they do want their weekly wages."

Every advocate of international peace must take these facts into account; for it is only too plain that the present daily life of peace for multitudes is not sufficiently attractive and full of meaning to evoke active support for its preservation. Economic and social issues are thus inextricably bound up with the issues of peace and war. Nevertheless, the main thesis of this chapter is not thereby invalidated. For the reaction of industrial distress upon a desire for war is psychological rather than economic in a direct and immediate sense; and it still remains true that the impulses associated with nationalism are the chief provocation to international strife. It is only, therefore, by keeping the economic and political factors distinct that we shall understand why the modern world is regimented for war; and in the light of that understanding we must proceed to ask how the violent passions of nationalism may be diverted into channels which make, not for the alleged glory of any particular people, but for the good of all mankind.

CHAPTER XII

THE DEFENSE OF NATIONALISM AND THE ILLUSION OF MILITARY SECURITY

ATTENTION has been drawn to the fact [1] that the world is today increasingly an interdependent unity, alike in material things and in things of the mind and the spirit. It is difficult to overrate the importance of this fact; for more than any other it determines our approach to international questions. Moreover, it is essentially a modern problem; for it is only in this twentieth century that the entire globe has been explored by mankind and its several parts each related to the others through an increasing multitude of contacts. This is most obvious in a physical sense; the internal combustion engine has made possible the motorcar and the aeroplane; wireless telegraphy and telephony, together with the radio, have canceled out time and distance; the prospect of television promises a still further extension of this process; the cinema brings the whole world before our eyes; the opening of the Panama Canal has removed the last obstacle to speedy marine transport, and the building of motor roads has brought the hinterlands of every continent into touch with civilization; scientific refrigeration applied to the carriage of food-

[1] See Chapter III.

stuffs enables the ends of the earth to contribute their products to every region, and mechanical skill in engineering has subdued forest and prairie and swamp to the service of man.   All these technical advances have effected a quiet and yet speedy revolution alike in action and in thought, of which the present generation is hardly aware.   At the time of the war between Great Britain and the United States in 1812, the British Orders in Council (which provoked the war by their assertion of the right to impress British sailors upon American ships for naval purposes) were repealed five days after the declaration of war by the American Senate, and before the news of the declaration reached England; moreover, the most important battle of the war was fought a couple of weeks after peace had been signed at Ghent.   But one hundred years later the news of the outbreak of the World War in 1914 actually reached Washington by the clock five hours before the outbreak occurred, and the cable has made any repetition of the tragic folly of 1812 quite impossible.   In the economic sphere everyone is familiar in these days with the immediate and world-wide repercussions of currency manipulation in any capital in the world; and a new invention in any department of manufacture has an almost instantaneous reaction on world prices or the value of stocks and shares.   Thirty years ago Mr. Frank Norris produced a trilogy of novels in which this economic interdependence was indicated, and since his day the facts which he outlined have become still more apparent to the man in the street; in *The Octopus*

Mr. Norris drew a picture of the wheatfields of the San Joaquin Valley in California, *The Pit* told of the cornering of the wheat market on the Chicago Exchange, and *The Wolf* pointed the moral by depicting the subsequent famine among wheat consumers in Italy. In the realm of political ideas the same rapid interdependence is observable; the reforms of Peter the Great in the seventeenth century were all but unknown by the world of his day, but the Russian Revolution instigated by Lenin in 1917 created an immediate reaction in every civilized country; less than a century ago East and West had practically no contacts, apart from occasional missionary enterprise and trading ventures, but today the depreciation of the Japanese yen throws world markets into confusion, and manufacturers everywhere have to readjust their activities to a new situation.

During the present century we have adjusted our domestic and industrial life to these newly created conditions to a far greater extent than is the case with political life, especially in its international aspect. In the political realm much of our thinking and a large part of our action is still governed by conceptions and traditions carried over from bygone days, when the world lived to a large degree in watertight compartments. The reasons for this will be considered later, but for the moment the fact itself needs to be stressed; for it is this which leads the nations without exception to meet the growing contacts of an interdependent world by an endeavor to preserve the national isolation which modern tendencies are so rapidly undermining. Economically this takes the form of tariffs and quotas and managed currencies, and even among economic experts who advise statesmen there is a persistent refusal to envisage the world as a single unit for purposes of production and distribution and consumption; the trail of nationalism is seen here as clearly as anywhere. But it is in the political sphere that nationalism persists in its most virulent form; for in every country on earth statesmen maintain what are called the "national defenses" in order that the state may be able to repel any possible assault upon its self-sufficient sovereignty. From this point of view, military preparedness becomes a sacred obligation of citizenship; and in consequence every nation builds up an ever more deadly arsenal of weapons for a war which no one desires but for which everyone prepares.

What needs to be realized, however, is that the facts of an interdependent world have made national isolation impossible, and modern statesmanship, therefore, which leans upon military preparedness is as much behind the times as a man who should endeavor to ship goods across the American continent in an old-time prairie-schooner instead of utilizing the methods of modern transport. The maze of concrete fortifications which the French government has built upon the Franco-German front since 1918 is no more up to date than is a hansom cab amid the motor traffic of London; but with this difference — the mind which still thinks in terms of national defense (whether by fortifications or naval superiority or by aerial squadrons) is not merely a back number but a public danger. Lord Salisbury knew the folly of the military mind when he said on one occasion that " if it were allowed full scope it would insist upon the importance of garrisoning the Moon in order to protect us from Mars." But even if it could achieve such lunacy, we should be not more secure but less so; for under modern conditions — as all the experts tell us — war cannot bring security to any combatant or group of combatants, but only disaster to all. As a means of defense, whether of territory or population or commerce or culture, modern war is worse than futile; and hence the ancient Roman doctrine, " If you wish for peace prepare for war," is no longer valid, if indeed it ever was.

In a short view it may be possible to give a certain limited justification to this doctrine. Rome, for instance, overawed the provinces by force of arms, and so maintained the *Pax Romana;* and in modern times it has been claimed that the mobilization of the British fleet in the English Channel in 1898 prevented the Fashoda incident from developing into a European war. Such incidents are a commonplace of history, but they are no final justification of the Roman dictum just quoted; for in the long view — as distinct from the short view — the attempt to ensure national security by military preparedness is an illusion and always miscarries. There are three principal reasons for this; for the idea that military preparedness makes for security ignores certain leading facts of life.

In the first place, the military-security thesis ignores

what for convenience of designation may be called psychological facts: and this is seen in the assumption behind all pleas for military defense that human nature can be permanently cowed and coerced by threats or force or economic pressure. The thesis, however, thereby maligns human nature, for it is not in the last analysis a craven composition, but is essentially heroic.

Christianity of course recognizes this heroic element when it places the cross at the heart of the gospel message. For the cross is not merely a point for theological disputation or a means of personal salvation: it embodies an ethical principle which applies as much to the salvation of society as of the individual; and this principle is expressed in the Christian demand for fidelity to the authority of Christ as the final means of saving the world from the sin of war, by meeting violence not with violence, but with its opposite. This process, however, obviously makes large demands upon the heroism of human nature, and is poles asunder from the militarists' assumption that men will perforce succumb to a display of force.

The story of Captain Oates in the Antarctic is typical of human nature in a desperate situation or when challenged by a critical moral choice: to step out into an Antarctic blizzard to certain death in order that one's comrades may have a chance of life has nothing of the drama of the battlefield about it, but it marked Captain Oates not only as "a verray parfit gentil knyght," but as a heroic exponent of Christian virtue. The glory of every battlefield lies not in its mutual slaughter, but in the multitude of those incidental heroisms by which the common soldier stands by his comrades or even retrieves a fallen enemy; the history of military struggle ought to convince every military-minded person that human nature may be broken but rarely bent by physical violence. It is this element of the heroic which gives such splendor to the resistance of the Maccabees to Antiochus, or the stubborn refusal of the Netherlanders to succumb to Spanish dominance, or in our own day the spontaneous reaction of Belgian manhood to the German invasion. An individual or a people may succumb to the threat of *force majeure* for the time being; but the whole history of the " balance of power " in Europe testifies to the fact that human nature, crushed at the outset by impotence, only awaits the opportunity for retaliation, and that sooner or later it makes this effective either by counter-preparation or by alliances. The reaction of modern Germany to the penal clauses of the Versailles Treaty, or the pre-war race in armaments, when Von Tirpitz sought to challenge the supremacy of the British navy, underlines this truth for the present generation; and in all history highly armed empires, from the days of Babylon and before down to Napoleon Buonaparte and Kaiser Wilhelm, have provoked their own downfall by stimulating the resistance of those they oppressed. It is a lesson which modern dictatorships must some day learn, unless in the meantime they accommodate their government to human psychology. If, therefore, psychological facts were given their due weight, it would be obvious to every observer

of events that armaments are always more of a provocation than a protection; for the insistence on military
security by one nation denies to others the security
which it demands for itself, and it asks others to accept an inferior position which itself refuses. It thereby
ignores elementary psychological facts.

But to no less an extent the military-security thesis
ignores political facts. The chief of these is the intimate relation between policy and armaments; for what
needs defense in the modern world is not primarily a
nation's territory but its policy; and therefore the key
to national security lies not with the War Department
but with the Foreign Office. It is not that nations want
war; on the contrary, the peoples everywhere wish for
peace and their statesmen continually echo this wish in
public utterances. But people and statesmen alike want
things which can only be secured or maintained by war
or by readiness for war; and it is this fact which underlines the relation between armaments and policy.

The point can be illustrated from contemporary
events. Great Britain, for instance, at the present moment is establishing a huge naval and aircraft base
at Singapore, and the enterprise is represented in the
British House of Commons as necessary for " the defense of the Empire." But this phrase is merely a cover
for the imperial policy which holds vast territories in
fee to the British Crown and retains the islands of the
seas as naval and commercial bases; moreover, no explanation of " defensive " activity at Singapore is adequate which ignores the " White Australia policy ";

indeed the Singapore base is more intimately associated with this policy than with anything else; for its purpose is not the defense of territory, except in so far as that territory may be endangered by a policy which necessarily provokes the resentment of oriental peoples. The principle of a " Red Indian North America," sparsely occupied by a few nomadic tribes, would have been as justifiable three centuries ago as is the claim of the Commonwealth of Australia today that, for all time its empty spaces shall remain vacant, while an all-white civilization digs itself in around the fringes of the island continent. No facile solution of the problem of oriental immigration can be prescribed; but it is too often forgotten that the alternative to the exclusion of the colored races is not necessarily their indiscriminate admission. For there is a middle term which is indicated by the word " regulation "; and an agreement with the oriental nations on terms of this kind would immediately ease the political situation in the Far East, relieve the anxieties of Antipodean statesmanship, and lift from the shoulders of Great Britain the burden of apprehension which today leads to the building of the Singapore base. It is a signal illustration of the intimate relation which exists between policy and armaments.

The same relationship may be seen wherever national armaments figure in the concerns of statecraft. French and Italian naval competition is directly due to the North African colonial policy of both powers, the one holding and the other coveting the northern littoral of the Dark Continent. On the other hand the peaceable policy of the Scandinavian countries requires no defense, and in consequence the Scandinavian peoples are not obsessed — as they were under the imperialism of Gustavus Adolphus in the seventeenth century — by the constant fear of armed invasion; from a military point of view Norway and Sweden are negligible factors, yet no countries on the face of the earth are at once more secure and more prosperous. Once again the facts point to the close relationship between armaments and policy; and it is this dominant political fact which the military-security thesis invariably ignores when it pleads the necessity of armed defense in the name of national security.

There is, however, another sense in which the plea for armed defense ignores political facts. For, while policy and armaments are counterparts and one is always the expression of the other, it by no means follows that a given policy can be made effective by military measures; and still less can moral aims be achieved by violence.[2] Yet this is the fallacy by which again and again the counsels of statecraft seem to be guided. For instance, responsible statesmen in every country at the outbreak of war in 1914 were full of pious and high-sounding assertions of moral aims which were to be achieved by force of arms; but one and all failed to realize that such aims can never be determined by the chance or mischance of military victory. Precisely in the measure that the aims of statecraft are moral, they

[2] Reference has already been made to this fact in Chapter I of Part II, above, where historical instances are given.

turn for their realization upon the willing response of
those who are concerned in their fulfilment; and this
willing response is the very thing which cannot be
postulated in those who are defeated in war; for, by
hypothesis, they needed to be coerced by force of arms
just because they refused to give the desired response
to the aims of the victors.

Mr. Asquith's famous declaration of British war
aims in August 1914 stands as an ironic commentary
upon the futility of military methods to vindicate moral
ideals. " We shall never," he said, " sheathe the sword
which we have not lightly drawn until Belgium re-
covers in full measure all, and more than all, that she
has sacrificed, until France is adequately secured against
the menace of aggression, until the rights of the smaller
nationalities of Europe are placed upon an unassailable
foundation, and until the military domination of Prussia is wholly and finally destroyed." The " sword "
then drawn has been " sheathed " since 1918; but where
are those steadfast and desirable consequences which
were to proceed from its use? Belgium is territorially
intact; but ask the widows and orphans, the bereaved
parents and lovers, the army of the unemployed, the
distracted business men, if Belgium has " recovered in
full measure all, and more than all, that she has sacrificed"! Does France, in spite of a crushing victory,
feel herself " adequately secured against the menace
of aggression "? Are the " smaller nationalities of Europe " assured of their place in the sun? In Germany
the " military domination of Prussia " has gone; but

a more evil and a more brutal despotism sits in its place. The "sword" was drawn, and for four and a half bitter and bloody years it was employed — according to the statesmen — in order to implement the high ideals of peace and democracy. But if there is one unassailable moral that remains, it is that the "sword" has failed to secure what in the relationships of spiritual beings can only be achieved by spiritual weapons.

Rupert Brooke labored under the same illusion as did the statesmen when he spoke for his generation in 1914:

> Honor has come back, as a king, to earth,
> And paid his subjects with a royal wage;
> And Nobleness walks in our ways again;
> And we have come into our heritage.

But Honor and Nobleness, which are, indeed, evoked by war, always wither under its blast; and the poet's lines therefore stand today as a mark of the tragic irony of unfulfilled ideals which always accompanies the effort to secure moral and political aims by force of arms.

The military-security thesis ignores psychological and political facts; but in these days it is also invalidated by physical facts. When we are told that it is necessary to defend our country from attack, there are always two underlying assumptions, neither of which is justified by the facts of life. The first assumption is that military defense will be *successful;* but obviously this can never be taken for granted; the defense may fail, and in that case the last state of the country will be worse than the first; for unsuccessful defense means a rear-guard action in which the enemy occupies and lays waste the country which he is invading. But a far more serious aspect of the case is the assumption that military defense is *possible;* in all the facile talk of those who plead for military preparedness the possibility of defending by force of arms is taken for granted. This of course is due to the unconscious and not unnatural habit of thinking of modern warfare in terms of wars that are passed; but in this respect we need to set our minds free from memories even so recent as those of 1914–18, for in the years which have followed the close of the World War mechanical and chemical invention has reconstituted every modern army that is capable of taking the field. The result is that with modern weapons, defense (and therefore the security of the territory defended) is a physical impossibility; and the only course open from a military point of view is counter-attack. A few quotations will substantiate this state-ment. Mr. Stanley Baldwin, speaking in the House of Commons on November 10, 1932, spoke as follows:

" The speed of air attack compared with the attack of an army, is as the speed of a motor car to that of a four-in-hand, and in the next war you will find that any town which is in reach of an aerodrome can be bombed within five minutes of war from the air, to an extent which was inconceivable in the last war; and the question will be whose morale will be shattered quickest by that preliminary bombing? I think it is well also for the man in the street to realize that there is no power on earth that can protect him from being bombed. Whatever people may tell him the bomber will always get through. *The only defense is in offense, which means that you will have to kill more women and children more quickly if you want to save yourselves* [italics by the author]. The amount of time that has been wasted at Geneva in discussing such questions as the reduction in size of aeroplanes, the prohibition of the bombardment of the civil population, the prohibition of bombing, has really reduced me to despair. . . . The prohibition of the bombardment of the civil population . . . is impracticable so long as any bombing exists at all."

This was followed by Lord Halsbury [3] in the House of Lords on December 14, 1932, who said:

" In regard to disarmament, they had to realize that a tiny amount of poison gas would completely obliterate London. Mr. Baldwin was right when he said there was no defense known against aircraft attack. London today is absolutely defenseless; so is Brussels and so is Berlin, and so is every big industrial town."

In reply to these observations Lord Hailsham, the Minister for War, spoke as follows on the same date:

[3] Lord Halsbury speaks with the authority of an expert chemist.

" It was impossible to devise any practical means of avoiding the horrors which Lord Halsbury had predicted in the next war."

What these statements mean in detail has been elaborated in a Report of a Commission appointed by the Inter-Parliamentary Union; the terms of reference were: " What would be the character of a new war? " That question was answered by no less than nineteen experts drawn from various countries and from various fields of activity connected with military science.[4] Their conclusions can be summarized as follows: [5]

The Great Powers dispose of from 1500 to 2000 war aeroplanes apiece, of which perhaps 30 per cent are bombers. . . . One chemical contributor estimates that a couple of machines, distributing a certain chemical, would suffice to put London out of a war. . . . Let us assume that a belligerent decides to employ 300 bombing machines against London. The service experts all admit that the majority of those 300 aeroplanes would get over London, possibly at a great height. They would be sent in waves. The first wave would carry high explosive, including individual bombs weighing a ton apiece. . . . A ton bomb will destroy a whole city block; it will wreck any subterranean shelter which is roofed with less than 80 feet of solid earth or 13 feet of reinforced concrete. The effect of the first wave

[4] The Report is published in book form under the title *What would be the Character of a New War?* and is published by Gollancz, London.

[5] Quoted from *The New Statesman and Nation,* January 2, 1932.

would be to drive the entire population underground, kill many thousands of people, and disorganize all public services, including food supplies. . . . On the heels of the first wave would arrive the second wave of raiders, dropping incendiary bombs filled with thermite, which burns at 3000 degrees centigrade, and cannot be put out by any known extinguisher. . . . They would multiply their frightful effects with the aid of broken gas mains and blazing petrol stores. The people, crouching underground, would soon be aware that over their heads London was a sea of flame. The final wave of raiders would drop poison gas and vesicant dew. The poison gas, being heavier than air, would penetrate the underground refuges, excepting those protected by airtight doors and supplied with pure filtered air by tall conduits protruding above the gas level in the blazing streets. The vesicant chemicals are so noxious that a man will die if three drops touch no more than his foot. . . . By a refinement of cruelty all these lethal substances can be dropped in containers fitted with time fuses, so that fresh outbreaks occur periodically, long after the raiders have departed.

Faced with this prospect of unprecedented catastrophe, the wisdom of modern statecraft can think of nothing better than gas-mask drill for the civilian population. The general public is to be officially encouraged to train themselves for self-defensive action in the event of an aerial attack: mothers will presumably be shown how to fit a gas mask on their babies, and fathers will be instructed in the rapid shepherding of the family as soon as the air-raid warning sounds! All this sounds too fanciful and even farcical to be accepted at its face value; yet Germany and Russia have already instituted these protective measures, and the British government on July 30, 1934, declared in the House of Commons that it was prepared to do likewise. The exact technique of defending civilians from attacking aircraft has been elaborated by the International Red Cross Society (whose headquarters are at Geneva) in seven recommendations issued in 1928, and among these are the following:

" *No. 3.* The building in every city of hermetically sealable subterranean chambers supplied with chemically produced oxygen or filtered air from a high chimney ventilation operated by a powerful motor. . . . These shelters should contain stocks of chemicals for neutralizing the atmosphere. . . . Food, water, and hospital stocks should be stored in each shelter in gas-proof receptacles, and the population should be warned that gas-contaminated water must be disinfected, boiling being insufficient for that purpose.

No. 5. All new buildings should be constructed with subterranean gas-proof shelters, separated from the superstructure and each other by masses of concrete.

No. 6. Municipalities should be warned that gas and water pipes must be laid deep under the ground.

No. 7. Each community should be provided with a

hermetically sealed van, with stores of oxygen, for removing the gassed." [6]

These measures apparently embody the quintessence of worldly wisdom in dealing with the menace of conflicting nationalisms; but they obviously demonstrate the bankruptcy of statesmanship in the presence of imminent world disaster. It is no wonder that Anthony Fokker, the designer of the German aeroplanes that raided England during the war, is of the opinion that " if the public rises to a realization of the nature of air warfare, it will turn against war altogether. That," he says, " is the only possible way to end the danger of war." Mr. Bernard Shaw, on the other hand, has declared with characteristic candor that in the event of an outbreak of hostilities he will immediately volunteer for the front-line trenches, since that will be the safest place in the world!

This description of modern warfare and the protective devices proposed is not quoted merely to stress the horrors which are in store for peoples whose faith is still fixed in military defense; the underlining of horror, indeed, generally defeats its own end; for horror induces fear, and fear leads to the very madness which produces the horrors of war. The present rulers of Germany are even exploiting the psychology of horror by erecting model air-bombs in the squares of Berlin and elsewhere in order to stimulate a demand for

[6] Quoted in *Chemical Warfare, its Possibilities and Probabilities*, by Elvira K. Fradkin, published by the Carnegie Endowment of International Peace, New York City.

national defense by rearmament; and recent aircraft maneuvers over New York and London respectively seem to have been definitely staged with a view to demonstrate the inadequacy of existing defenses, in order that the plea for a larger air-force might secure the assent of a terrified public opinion. The Christian reaction to the horrors of war will be dealt with in a later chapter; but meantime we are concerned only with the futility of war as a means of defending a nation or establishing security. Yet " defense " is the supreme benefit which political apologists invariably claim for military preparedness. The motto of the Navy League in Great Britain is " Defense not Defiance," and a plea for aggressive warfare receives short shrift from public opinion everywhere in the world. To that extent we can register a definite moral advance upon previous generations. But what if war itself can no longer " defend "? The military-security thesis breaks upon the physical facts of modern warfare. The day is not far behind us when it was possible to defend the territorial integrity of a country by fighting for it; but today the patriot who desires to defend his country will refuse to fight; for fighting means not the victory of one side and the defeat of the other, but the common ruin of both combatants and the mutual destruction of their common civilization. In other words, peace-at-any-price is the only way of security or defense; patriotism and prudence and pacifism are now one and the same. Even in the war of 1914–18 this moral could be deduced; the city of Brussels was undefended and therefore unharmed; on the other hand, Antwerp was defended and therefore destroyed. But events and processes have moved with incredible speed since 1914, and under modern conditions of warfare the story of Antwerp would be intensified and multiplied wherever the contending forces engaged in combat.

Many people are inclined to discount the estimates of experts in regard to the " character of a new war "; but even when the utmost allowance has been made for exaggeration or false anticipations, nothing can dispose of the final inability of military methods to do the only thing which is their alleged justification. For they are no longer capable of defending the country which employs them, or of offering security to the beleaguered populations who maintain them at so ruinous a cost.

The military theory of security by armaments is, therefore, an illusion; for the interdependence of the modern world makes national isolation ridiculous; and the facts of life — psychological, political, physical — make armed defense futile and bring disaster upon every nation which seeks to preserve its sovereignty by the processes of war.

CHAPTER XIII

THE ALTERNATIVE TO NATIONALISM

CONTACT between nation-states leads inevitably from time to time to a clash of purpose and policy; and these clashes — when inflamed by the emotions born of rival nationalisms — issue in competitive armaments, whose purpose is to safeguard the integrity of each nation against the others and to " defend " both the soil and the interests — commercial and other — of each separate nationality. But it is just here that nationalism threatens the very things which it professes to defend. For the " offensive " weapons of modern warfare have so far outrun the capacity for military defense as to make protection against armed attack a physical impossibility in any conflict between first-class powers. This is obviously the *reductio ad absurdum* of the nationalistic thesis of security by force of arms; and it is imperative, therefore, not only from a Christian standpoint, but no less from the standpoint of worldly wisdom, to find an alternative to nationalism which shall allow humanity to face its problems without the constant menace of mutual suicide through the outbreak of war. Western peoples are apt to smile at the oriental custom according to which the injured party in a dispute, as a means of revenge, commits suicide upon his opponent's doorstep. But the demand of the world's nationalisms that an injured or outraged people, or one which imagines itself outraged, must of necessity go to war in order to avenge or rectify the injustice is, from a practical point of view, no different from this oriental code of honor. If the peoples everywhere were not bound by antiquated military traditions (no longer relevant to modern life), the nationalist's cry of "defense" would be met by universal laughter, and armies and navies would dissolve in the ridicule of mankind.

The alternative to nationalism is not in these days a matter of theory or speculation; for there are already in existence political structures which exemplify what is required. The best known of these is the United States of America, where forty-eight separate and quasi-sovereign states are bound in a federal union. The sense of nationality or local patriotism is still vigorous in every one of the several states, and the popular nicknames for the states help to keep this alive; a native of the " Pine Tree State " would feel insulted if he were mistaken for a citizen of the " Blue Grass State," and one who cherishes his lineage in the " Bay State " will proudly assert his superiority over a parvenu from the "Golden State." Nevertheless — as indicated in a previous chapter — there is an essential difference between nationality and nationalism; and the local loyalties, therefore, which lead to pride of statehood, are all of them subordinate to the wider loyalty, symbolized by the forty-eight stars in the all-inclusive American flag.

Yet the era of competing and antagonistic nationalisms is not very far behind in American history. The Civil War of 1861–65 brought these into life for a brief period and revealed to all the world the kind of experience from which federalism has — but that for one disastrous episode — saved the American people. For, prior to the Declaration of Independence in 1776, the relation between certain of the thirteen colonies was not unlike that which prevails between the rival nationalisms of Europe or of South America today. Each colony had its own army, each had power to penalize the trade of its neighbor by tariffs, each was divided from the others by religious feeling: there were Independents in New England, Catholics in Maryland, Episcopalians in Virginia, Quakers in Pennsylvania; some of the colonies had differing economic interests, for the wealth of Georgia was in slaves and of New York in shipping; they had different national origins: there were English in Massachusetts and Virginia, Dutch in New York, Germans in Pennsylvania, Swedes in Delaware; and each, therefore, had strong local and historical sentiment of a nationalistic kind. Moreover, these rivalries were not overcome without difficulty; [1]

[1] The difficulties encountered by the federalists in the early days of the American Republic are indicated by every reliable historian of the United States. Compare the following picture of conditions in 1783.

" The dignified entreaties of Washington, the unanswerable reasoning of Hamilton, failed to move the minds of the citizens. . . . Rather than abandon their mean jealousies, their rivalries at once sordid and malicious, rather than part with, or delegate, a single shred of local sovereignty to clothe the shivering and naked form of federal government, the states fell one upon the other; each at the beginning looking merely for advantage to indeed the long struggle between state sovereignty and the principle of federalism is still reflected in the respective bias of the leading political parties. It was principally through the genius of Alexander Hamilton that federalism won the day; for it was he who secured the inclusion in the United States Constitution of those articles which provide for free trade within the Union,[2] the abolition of state armies,[3] and a Supreme Court for the adjudication of interstate disputes.

On different lines, and of a somewhat looser texture, the British Commonwealth of Nations has repeated the experience of the United States. Beginning with the British North America Act of 1867, the power of imperial control has gradually been weakened until, by the Statute of Westminster in 1926, the Dominions were given legal existence as " autonomous Communities within the British Empire, equal in status, in no

---

itself in injury to its neighbors, but as time went on, seeking injury to its neighbors even as an end desirable in itself. . . . The states with seaports preyed upon their land-locked brethren and provoked a boycott in return. Pennsylvania attacked Delaware. Connecticut was oppressed by Rhode Island and New York. New Jersey, lying between New York on the one hand and Pennsylvania on the other, was compared to a cask tapped at both ends; North Carolina, between South Carolina and Virginia, to a patient bleeding at both stumps. . . . The barbarities of the Pennsylvanians under Patterson outdid even the legend of British atrocities, and left a rankling memory in Connecticut. At one time war between Vermont, New Hampshire and New York seemed all but inevitable." *Alexander Hamilton; an Essay on American Union*, by Frederick S. Oliver, pp. 134 ff.

Substitute the countries of western Europe for Vermont, New Hampshire and New York, and we pass at once from 1783 to the present time.

[2] *United States Constitution*, Art. 1., Sec. 8.

[3] *Ibid.*, Art. 1, Secs. 8 and 10.

way subordinate one to another in any aspect of their domestic or external affairs, though united by a common allegiance to the Crown, and freely associated as members of the British Commonwealth of Nations." [4]

The important point to be observed is that, in both instances — whether in the United States or in the British Commonwealth — war between the component parts of these federal unions no longer enters into the calculations of statesmanship. The War Department in Washington does not draft strategic plans for the coercion of New Jersey or Iowa or Oregon; nor does the War Office in London pigeonhole schemes for the invasion of New Zealand or Canada by British armies. Disputes may arise between the several states or dominions as the case may be, but these are invariably referred in the one case to the Supreme Court at Washington, and in the other to the Judicial Committee of the Privy Council sitting as a court of law in the House of Lords in London.

Furthermore, it is to be observed that this substitution of federalism for nationalism has occurred without first of all revolutionizing the economic structure of the respective federal units; interstate warfare has been outlawed within the context of a capitalistic order and without a prior solution of economic problems. Thereby, indeed, the economic problems of the United States and of the British Commonwealth can be dealt with on a federal basis instead of, as previously, only within

[4] *Official Report of the Inter-Imperial Relations Committee* appointed by the Imperial Conference in London, 1926.

the restricted limits of each state or province. In other words, the solution of economic problems follows upon and does not precede the solution of the international problem.

It is interesting in this connection to contrast Central America and South America with the great republic of North America. To an even greater degree than in the United States, the Central and South American Republics enjoy the benefit of a common language and a common law; for every country south of the Rio Grande is either ex-Spanish or ex-Portuguese, while in North America the territories were colonized by countries as diverse in culture and outlook as Holland, France, Spain and Britain. Also in the Spanish-American Republics the prevailing religion everywhere is Roman Catholic, in sharp contrast to the divided religious allegiance of the citizens of the United States. Moreover, economic interests do not clash more in the one case than in the other; Chile and Peru have come to loggerheads over nitrates, Bolivia and Paraguay over oil, and in both instances the issue has led to protracted and cruel warfare. But these economic disputes have not been more bitter than the historic quarrel between West Virginia and Pennsylvania in regard to coal, or between the eastern and western states in regard to the monetization of silver; yet the last-named issues were settled by processes of law instead of by the arbitrament of war. In almost every respect the South American Republics had less to divide them, whether from a material or spiritual point of view, than had the several states of the American Union; but the absence of the federal principle and the preservation unimpaired of national sovereignty has made war as much a feature of South American history as it has been of European.

In the light of this contrast it is obvious that the alternative to the danger of nationalism is in some form of internationalism, by which the nations of the world shall be federated in regard to all those things which concern their common life. Internationalism, however, must be sharply distinguished from cosmopolitanism. Mr. H. G. Wells, in his book, *The Shape of Things to Come,* makes a strong plea for a World-State; but he strikes a cosmopolitan note which hardly does justice to the value of nationality and which tends to ignore the genius of each nation and race in favor of an undifferentiated uniformity. The aim of internationalism, on the other hand, is to preserve local and national differences, and yet prevent those differences breaking out into the discord of war. True love of country, indeed, no more conflicts with world interests than does love of one's family with the wider interests of the community in which we dwell; and the patriot therefore can encourage a wise internationalism without any suspicion of disloyalty to the interests of his native land. Dr. Johnson misunderstood patriotism when he defined it as " the last refuge of a scoundrel." The same is true of Mr. H. L. Mencken, who has declared in the pages of *The American Mercury* that he is " against Patriotism because it demands the acceptance of propositions which are obviously imbecile, such as that an American Presbyterian is the equal of Anatole France, Brahms or Ludendorff." These strictures, however, confuse patriotism with nationalism; for nationalism means an attitude of mind and feeling which gives to the nation a loyalty which properly belongs to humanity, and its typical expression is a belief that the sovereign state is something over which there can be no jurisdiction and beyond which there is no authority. The nationalist creed is expressed in the familiar formula, " My country right or wrong "; and hence, according to the nationalist, the citizen owes a supreme and unqualified allegiance to the state of which he is a member, and — as we see in Russia and Germany and Italy today — no ethical considerations can be set above what Machiavelli called " reasons of state." It need hardly be said, however, that this nationalist creed is a flagrant contradiction of the Christian outlook, which sees " peoples of every tribe and nation and tongue " retaining their respective cultures, and yet unified in a commonwealth where the culture of each shall contribute to the larger life of all.

So then patriotism and internationalism are both implicit in the federal structure of the United States and of the British Commonwealth; and this same blending of the local and the universal has now taken practical and world-wide shape in the establishment of the League of Nations. As such it registers a recoil from war which in the end, if properly cherished, will spell the abolition of competitive armaments.

Criticisms are often leveled against the League on the ground that it has failed to prevent war, and that the spirit of nationalism is still rampant. Both criticisms have substance, though not always to the extent that the critics suppose; for since 1920 the action of the League has actually composed a number of international disputes which contained within them the possible seeds of another world conflict,[5] and in certain cases it has actually caused hostilities to cease even after the guns had opened fire.[6] But it needs to be remembered that the League is only about fifteen years old, and it has usually taken much longer than this for a newly tried political instrument to become completely effective.

The United States Constitution adopted in 1789 is a case in point. It was with the utmost difficulty at first that its loyal observance was secured: questions of tariffs and state debts and foreign policy led to frequent talk of secession by some of the states; and indeed it required all the tact which even George Washington could command to preserve the unity of the Republic in its early years. But no one now pleads that because at

[5] The crisis between Italy and Greece in 1923 is the most notable of these; and there is little doubt that, without the League, the dispute over the Mosul boundary between Great Britain and Turkey in 1925 would not have been settled without a resort to arms.

[6] The leading cases are those of Poland and Lithuania in 1920, Jugo-Slavia and Albania in 1921, and Greece and Bulgaria in 1925. Moreover, but for the existence of the League, the Japanese seizure of Manchuria in 1932 would in all probability have led to an international scramble for the general partition of China into " spheres of influence " under the several powers.

certain points or on certain occasions the United States Constitution has proved ineffective it should therefore be abandoned and the forty-eight states lapse into their pre-1776 separatisms. The same applies to the League of Nations: in the main it is true to say — in every case of alleged failure — that what has been at fault is not the League of Nations but the nations of the League. In so far as the League has been unsuccessful, this is not an evidence that the Covenant of the League is unworkable, but only that — after a few years' endeavor to commend a new international instrument — the public opinion of the several countries signatory to the Covenant is still not emancipated from the agelong tradition of self-sufficient nationalism and the fetish of state sovereignty. The remedy, therefore, is not — as enemies of the League allege — to " scrap the League," but to utilize it and marshal public opinion behind it until resort to the League becomes as habitual and automatic in disputes and difficulties between nations as, in the case of personal differences, resort to courts and parliaments is normal between individual citizens. How to encourage and facilitate this process is a question which requires a chapter to itself;⁷ but in essence the problem is one of dealing with the emotions which today gather about nationalism and transferring them to the internationalism for which the League of Nations stands. That this can be done is manifest if we take account of the way in which, as communities expanded from a narrow tribal economy, local patriotisms

⁷ See closing chapter in this book,

were progressively changed into national patriotism. In the days of the Heptarchy from the fifth to the eighth centuries A.D., there were rival nationalisms on the soil of England and patriotism was bounded by the frontiers of Wessex or Mercia or Northumbria, as the case might be: with King Egbert came the unification of the seven kingdoms, and patriotism adjusted itself to the larger entity; in a similar way — if we follow the centuries through — the emotions of British nationalism expanded step by step until they covered first the whole of Great Britain and then the British Isles; and finally — since 1926 — British nationalism has willingly become surbordinate to the demands of imperial loyalty. The same story could be told of every people which has changed tribalism into nationhood or statehood into federation; and we are therefore fully in line with historic development when we plead for the sublimation of national loyalties into a world-loyalty, whose form and fealty shall be either the existing League of Nations (completed by the inclusion of all countries) or some other and better association of peoples, if and when such can be devised. Taking things as they are, however, the League at Geneva is the best existing approximation in practical politics to the ideal of a federated world; and the Christian, therefore, can make an effective contribution to peace by throwing the whole weight of his citizenship on the side of the internationalism for which the League stands.

It is not necessary here to embark upon a detailed description of the constitution of the League or of the many significant achievements which already stand to its credit.[8] In its campaign against chattel-slavery, through its Health Commission and the control of international quarantine, by its dealing with the problems of war refugees, the traffic in dangerous drugs, the white-slave traffic, the control and advancement of "backward peoples" under the Mandates Commission, the administration of disputed areas like Danzig and the Saar, by its protection of minorities, its financial reconstruction of bankrupt nationalities, its organization of transit and communications on a world-wide scale, its codification of international law, its registration of treaties, its Court of International Justice at The Hague, its Committee on Intellectual Co-operation, and in numerous other ways the League has become in a few short years an indispensable agent of civilized intercourse. For the League exists to deal with problems of human relationship which concern more than one nation, and which, if not dealt with by an international organization, would lead to universal disaster. Very few people realize how rapidly, in spite of the insurgence of rabid nationalisms, international co-operation is gaining ground by the sheer necessity of world interdependence; and one can say, therefore, of the League what the rationalist Voltaire said of the Deity: "If there were no League of Nations it would be necessary to invent one."

[8] Those who wish for information under these heads can consult the excellent literature issued by the National Council for Prevention of War, 532 Seventeenth Street, N. W., Washington, D. C.

The constitutional organs of the League — the Assembly, the Council, and the permanent Commissions — correspond roughly in parliamentary nomenclature to the House of Commons and the Cabinet, together with the Committees associated with each. But the most important feature of the League is not the constitutional procedure by which it carries on its work at Geneva, but the fact that — in the lobbies and precincts of the Assembly Hall and on hotel terraces — the official representatives of more than fifty nations rub shoulders, offer each other cigarettes, sip coffee together, laugh at the same jests, respond to the same human appeal. This is already a familiar process in the modern world; but we need only to turn to the official documents on the origin of the World War to see what a revolution the League of Nations has already made in the diplomatic methods of the pre-war era. In those days diplomacy worked with rare exceptions solely through ambassadorial channels, and the result was cumbrous to the last degree; the process indeed can be expressed in a revised version of " The House that Jack Built," which would stand like this:

This is the Secretary for Foreign Affairs.
This is the Dispatch which was written by the Secretary for Foreign Affairs.
This is the Courier who conveyed the Dispatch.
This is the Ambassador who received the Courier.
This is the Chancellor who gave an audience to the Ambassador.

This is the Report which was made by the Chancellor.
This is the Cabinet which adopted the Report.
And finally: This is the Monarch (or President) who
was advised by the Cabinet, which adopted the Report, which was made by the Chancellor, who gave
an audience to the Ambassador, who received the
Courier, who conveyed the Dispatch, which was
written by the Secretary for Foreign Affairs.

The whole of this sevenfold process was then reversed
through an infinite gradation of formalities, until at
last the Secretary for Foreign Affairs received a be-
lated and generally out-of-date reply to the dispatch
which he had originally written. This is no caricature
of pre-war diplomatic processes; and if the League of
Nations has done nothing else except establish a new
tradition in diplomacy which brings foreign ministers
face to face at regular intervals, it would be worth all
the labor expended upon it;[9] for when statesmen gather
at Geneva, they discover that every nation is plagued
with problems common to them all and which, because common to all, can only be solved by common
effort.

What is wrong with the world today is not — as
the critics of the League declare — the " interference "
of Geneva with the affairs of the several nations, but
contrariwise the absence of the spirit of Geneva in the
public opinion of the nations themselves. That fact,

[9] It is customary nowadays at the Annual Assembly of the League
for at least half of the nations represented to include their Prime Minister
or their Foreign Minister in the official delegation; the actual figures for
the Assembly of 1933 were 8 Prime Ministers and 24 Foreign Ministers.

indeed, indicates the real obstacle to the success of the League of Nations, for it implies the persistence of a traditional belief in national sovereignty; and this means in practice the assertion by each nation of the right to do just as it will — in regard to peace and war, tariffs and quotas, imperial adventure and economic penetration — entirely regardless of the rights and interests of other peoples. The League, therefore, can never be an effective instrument of international peace until national sovereignty gives way to the wider sovereignty of the World Parliament at Geneva in all matters of international concern. Such acceptance of League authority, however, means a radical change in the popular outlook upon international affairs; and for this most people are not yet ready. The popular attitude of mind is not inaptly indicated by the remark attributed to a well-known senator at Washington, who registered his objection by declaring that " the United States could not possibly join the League now that all these foreigners were in it "! That remark, whether true or apocryphal, emphasizes the supreme need for the cultivation of an international mind. In other words, the problem of world peace at bottom is neither political nor economic, but psychological and spiritual; for it depends upon the point of view which sees the foreigner not as a potential enemy or even as a competitor, but as a friend whose widest interests coincide with our own. The all-important task, therefore, before the patriotic citizen of every country is not — as the nationalist asserts — to learn how to fight, but to discover how to co-operate in an interdependent world.

CHAPTER XIV

NATIONALISM AND DISARMAMENT

The Factors Which Prevent Disarmament

If the reader has been convinced by the argument of the preceding chapters, he will be ready to agree that armed nationalisms are the begetters of war and that some form of international organization is the only guarantee of world peace. But international organization means of necessity a qualification of national sovereignty, and it implies a restriction upon the generally acknowledged claim that any given nation may legitimately vindicate what it deems to be its rights or its interests by a resort to war. For the whole essence of international organization is that nations shall do by law and agreement what hitherto they have sought to do by force. The corollary, therefore, of an international order is national disarmament. This is well understood by statesmen. When, after the World War, the Allies sought to guarantee peace in Europe, they forbade the possession of aggressive arms to Germany and established certain demilitarized zones between Germany and France; also they solemnly declared, in a memorandum addressed to Germany[1] and in the

---

[1] The Memorandum is dated June 1919, and it assures the German government that German disarmament is " the first step toward the reduction and limitation of armaments " by all nations. Part 5 of the Treaty of Versailles also affirms the intention of the victorious Allies to initiate " a general limitation of the armaments of all nations."

Covenant of the League of Nations,[2] that world peace and disarmament go hand in hand.

Yet, despite these assertions and despite the overwhelming desire for peace on the part of the peoples everywhere, the world's nationalisms continually thwart the efforts of the League of Nations, and national armaments are everywhere on the increase. What then is the explanation of this apparent contradiction of purpose? Why is it that disarmament delays and nationalism is still vigorous? Two factors explain the situation: one is military tradition and the other is national policy; and in regard to both, the Christian citizen has a specific contribution to make toward world peace.

Military tradition is far more deeply rooted in the popular mind than is generally recognized. No sane person in any country wants war for its own sake, but the illusion still persists that in the last issue a nation can only be defended by force of arms. As has been shown in a previous chapter,[3] the application of chemistry and aeronautics to warfare has, since the close of the war of 1914–18, made defense dependent not upon a readiness to fight but upon a refusal to fight; so that today, even for prudential reasons and in the name of national security, unilateral disarmament on the part of any nation is a far better defense than armies and navies and air forces; a people is infinitely safer in a

[2] Article 8 declares that " the maintenance of peace requires the reduction of national armaments to the lowest point consistent with national safety and the enforcement by common action of international obligations."
[3] Chapter V.

physical sense with no armaments than with big armaments. But statesmen and people alike, even when they are aware of the illusion of military security, are still governed by agelong tradition rather than by the light of reason; for tradition touches the emotions and enlists historic memories and is part of the social environment of the citizen in the modern state. Consequently, most of the unconscious or subconscious influences of citizenship and many of the customs of our common life suggest the value of military power, despite the fact that such power is nowadays a boomerang which must inevitably destroy the people who use it. Modern psychology no less than human experience has made us familiar with the tendency of emotion to discount the intellect, and it is this tendency which gives military tradition its hold upon the popular imagination, long after the tradition has ceased to correspond with the realities of international life.

This military tradition is buttressed in numberless ways, and in any civilized community it is all but impossible to escape its influence. The teaching of history in our schools plays a major part in this process; for though the League of Nations Committee on Intellectual Co-operation is seeking to secure an international emphasis in the history books of all countries, yet the soldier is still magnified as the hero *par excellence,* and " dying for one's country " (which in the actual practice of war always means " killing for one's country ") is represented as something far nobler than living for one's country. The pageantry of state is another fac-

tor behind the facile acceptance of military tradition.
The opening of the British Parliament, the funeral of
the French President, even Armistice Day celebrations,
are invariably associated with marching and counter-
marching of troops, whose weapons emphasize the fact
that preparation for war is one of the chief departments
of governmental activity; every person of note who
comes on any kind of official business to Great Britain
undertakes as his first and formal duty the placing of
a wreath on the Cenotaph in Whitehall; the young
King of Siam (who was hardly weaned when the war
occurred) and the Australian cricketers (whose only
knowledge of warfare is a test match), no less than
the French Prime Minister or a Dominion Premier,
invariably conform to custom and express their sorrow
for the fallen by this conventional rite. A permanent
military guard keeps sentry-go before the tomb of the
Unknown Warrior in Washington. The obscure
heroes of peace, who gave their lives in a mine disaster
or in saving the victims of a wreck, are " unwept, un-
honored and unsung," but the heroes of battle are belauded as though national greatness and military glory
were one and the same.

Richard Le Gallienne in a few telling lines has shown
how even the most peace-loving citizen can be swept
into a current of dangerous emotion by such pageantry:

> War I abhor; and yet how sweet
> The sound along the marching street
> Of drum and fife. And I forget

Wet eyes of widows, and forget
Broken old mothers, and the whole
Dark butchery without a soul.

Without a soul — save this bright drink
Of heady music, sweet as death;
And even my peace-abiding feet
Go marching with the marching street.

For yonder, yonder, goes the fife,
And what care I for human life?
The tears fill my astonished eyes
And my full heart is like to break;
And yet 'tis all embannered lies,
A dream those little drummers make.

O, it is wickedness to clothe
Yon hideous grinning thing, that stalks
Hidden in music, like a queen
That in a garden of glory walks,
Till good men love the thing they loathe!

Art! thou hast many infamies,
But not an infamy like this.
O snap the fife and still the drum,
And show the monster as he is!

But there are other factors than public pageantry
which thus minister to popular illusion in regard to
war. Monuments and memorials to those killed in

battle adorn every city square and many a village green: battleflags adorn the cathedrals, and church parades periodically emphasize the blessing which official Christianity still bestows upon men of war. The writer has in his possession a photograph of a gun standing above the chancel steps and right in front of the altar of St. Paul's Cathedral in London: the occasion was a parade of one of the artillery regiments; but it meant that the congregation could only worship the Prince of Peace by bowing before an instrument of war.[4]

The uncritical use of the Old Testament in Christian worship and sermons which reflect this " Old Testament Christianity " have not a little to do with the maintenance of military tradition. Captured guns and tanks are placed in public parks, and the passerby regards them as a mark of the prowess of his countrymen.[5] Statuary is another means by which military tradition is buttressed in the public mind; and every capital in Europe gives the place of honor to known and unknown gentlemen in soldier's uniform, either standing with hand on sword or precariously poised

---

[4] Lest this episode be dismissed as incredible, the exact details together with a photograph of the gun *in situ,* may be found in *No More War,* the official publication of the British No More War Movement under date August 1923.

[5] There is an exception to this rule at Eckington in Derbyshire, where the following inscription has been placed upon a German gun at the edge of the village green:

" This gun has been placed here to remind the people of Eckington of the vicious folly of war which has been responsible for the deaths of so many of the best of them, and in the hope that the ugliness of the object will impress the children so that they will grow up with a natural hatred of war and the brutal machinery that accompanies it."

upon a prancing steed. Moreover, every country has its popular songs or national anthems, which exalt the military virtues or associate national greatness with military victory. The second stanza of the British national anthem is rarely sung nowadays, but it is typical of the invariable association of nationalism with militarism, when it commends the monarch to the mercies of God in the following words:

> O Lord our God arise,
> Scatter his enemies
> And make them fall.
> Frustrate their knavish tricks,
> Confound their politics,
> On Thee our hopes we fix.
> God save us all.

Even the first verse, which is sung on all public occasions of a national character, includes the prayer to Almighty God to " send him victorious, happy and glorious." The American national anthem celebrates one of the most discreditable and least glorious episodes in Anglo-American relationships; it presumes to describe the war of 1812–14, and its second verse does so in the following terms:

Oh, where is that host who so vauntingly swore
That the fury of war and the battle's confusion
A home and a fireside would leave us no more?
Their blood has wiped out their foul footsteps' pollution.
No refuge could save the hireling and slave

From the terror of flight and the gloom of the grave.
The star-spangled banner, oh long may it wave
O'er the land of the free and the home of the brave.

In these ways, and in a multitude of others, the subtle
suggestion is continually playing upon the mind of
young and old alike that the glory and greatness of a
nation is somehow dependent on the power to defeat
an enemy upon the field of battle. But this suggestion
is a libel upon all that is best in every nation. The fact
that it glosses over the bestial character of modern
warfare increases its sinister influence upon the popular outlook and adds to those illusions which cause
the public in general to acquiesce in the institution of
war as a legitimate if regrettable form of international
relationship. It is this traditional belief in the efficacy
and legitimacy of war which paralyzes the demand for
disarmament; and the spell of this military tradition,
therefore, must somehow be broken if the modern
world would escape the tyranny of armaments.

It is here that the Christian faith is especially potent:
for it meets tradition on its own ground by opposing
to the emotions of nationalism the finer emotions which
enlist human energy in devotion to the Person of Jesus.
To those seized by that devotion war is a denial of their
most cherished loyalty, and for them the glory of a
nation is registered not in the mass enmities of battle,
but in reflecting the character of One who dared to
suffer rather than inflict suffering, and who killed
enmity by loving the enemy. To embody that reaction,

therefore, and to express it in his citizenship, alike by speech and by action, is an essential element of the Christian's contribution to peace.

This is also true of the second of the two factors which today maintain the temper of nationalism. This second factor is national policy. The relation between policy and armaments has already been indicated,[6] and from this point of view, therefore, the key to disarmament is to be found in the adoption of a peaceable policy which needs no military defense because it provokes in other nations neither resentment nor aggressive desire.

The statesmen of every nation are loud in their assertion that they and their respective peoples do not want war, and there is no reason to suspect the *bona fides* of such assertion's. But they pursue policies or they maintain a situation which can only be implemented by readiness for war: and it is this which accounts for the general unwillingness — at least among the great powers — to take risks in the direction of disarmament. For disarmament as an ideal, modern statesmanship has no praise too lavish; but it insists invariably that the scrapping of navies or the disbanding of army corps shall leave the existing balance of power unaltered. In the jargon of the day, disarmament must be multilateral, not unilateral. Lord Cecil exactly expressed the irony of the situation when he said, " Disarmament is like a social function: no one wants to arrive until everyone is there! "

[6] Chapter V.

Change of policy, therefore, is the price of disarmament, and *vice versa* effective disarmament would have an immediate and inevitable reaction upon policy. Statesmen the world over are, of course, well aware of this; but it is not generally recognized by the world-public, and it is no unusual thing, therefore, for ordinary citizens to express a desire for the limitation or reduction of armaments, and at the same time assure their hearers that they have no wish to see any diminution in the prestige of the British Empire or — if they happen to be American citizens — to involve the United States in world affairs. In other words, the international *status quo* is to remain as it is, with nationalisms unimpaired. But what people fail to recognize is that the *status quo* is what it is, and the British Empire and the United States occupy their present position in world affairs by reason of the existing disposition of armaments among the nations of the world, and especially among the great powers. The world of today — with its frontiers imposed by conquest, its imperial territories acquired and held by force of arms, its economic rivalries supported by tariffs and subsidies, its racial discriminations enforced by strategic advantage — all this rests at bottom upon equipment for war. That is to say, armaments exist, on the one hand, to maintain present international divisions, and on the other, to alter the present alignment in accordance with the ambitions or grievances of disgruntled nationalisms. They are an expression of policy.

Here, once again, the Christian citizen has a specific

contribution to make to the cause of world peace; for the gospel calls Christ's disciples to put fidelity to him first and everything else second. " If any man," said Jesus, " love father or mother, son or daughter — and we may rightly add nation or empire — more than me, he is not worthy to be my disciple." But if the will of God, as seen in Jesus, is " peace on earth," it follows that the Christian disciple will be prepared to surrender even the power and prestige of national sovereignty in pursuit of that ideal. In other words, he will be willing, as an expression of his Christian discipleship, to pay the price of peace, whatever that price may be in terms of national policy.

This may seem a small thing to do, when stated as a general principle. But when reduced to terms of practical politics, it will be seen that the Christian demand touches patriotic sentiment on the raw and conflicts at a score of points with the traditions and presuppositions which govern national life. For the risks of disarmament (concerning which we are so often warned) are not the risks of actual invasion, but the danger and damage which would ensue to national prestige and power, to the ability to dominate, to dictate, to do as one will in international affairs — all of which are included in the emotions of nationalism. It is these things which must be surrendered as the price of world peace; and for this surrender the Christian genius is peculiarly fitted. It is here, therefore, that we envisage once again the Christian's contribution to peace.

CHAPTER XV

NATIONALISM AND DISARMAMENT
The Changes Which Would Accompany
Disarmament

IN GENERAL, the effect of disarmament would be to
qualify national sovereignty: for an unarmed nation
would have no power to be a " law unto itself ";
nationalism therefore would be subordinate to international order. But these general effects would be expressed through certain definite changes in the mutual
relationship of nations which can be indicated under
four heads or divisions. These are not presented as an
exhaustive analysis, but only as indicating the kind of
thing that would necessarily be associated with disarmament.

The first — and in some respects the most important
— of these is the abolition of the prevailing distinction
between great powers and little nations. That distinction today rests to a large extent — though by no
means entirely — upon mere weight of gun metal.
When Japan, towards the end of the nineteenth century, determined to count as a " great power," this was
where she placed the emphasis; and her due reward
was the world's recognition of her right to sit in the
seats of the mighty. It would not be accurate to suggest that military reorganization was the sole element

in the situation; for the military capacity of modern Japan is closely associated with her economic development, and that in its turn arose from the insight and courage of men who deliberately defied outworn national traditions and led the people along new and unaccustomed paths.   But the fact remains that Japan's present significance in international affairs is due more to her armaments than to any other single factor; and the same is true of every one of the so-called " great powers " in the world of today.   Obviously, therefore, this status of greatness — in so far as it rests upon armed equipment — would disappear with any effective measure of disarmament.   But thereby the world would lose nothing that is of real worth; for the distinction between great powers and little nations has no relation whatever to essential human values.   Indeed it is true to say that human values invariably suffer when a nation aspires to the position of a great power: preoccupation with the apparatus of military " defense " of necessity diverts the national resources from socially constructive purposes to purposes of mutual destruction, and the maintenance of warlike equipment gathers to itself the energies which would otherwise be devoted to the culture of mind and body and the enfranchisement of the human spirit.   It is not accidental that the great empires of history have all of them finally gone down in ruin, or that nationalism invariably leads to the crushing of individuality under a regime of military regimentation.   The intolerance of modern European dictatorships toward any semblance of liberty is but the reverse of that tendency whose obverse is seen in the universal adoption of a military uniform as the sign and symbol of national greatness. At the time of the Boer War (1899–1902) Mr. L. T. Hobhouse drew attention to the significance of " little nations," and his words in this connection are worth quoting:

A great Imperialist [1] once coupled the name of " Little England " with the policy of surrender. It was a libel. . . . The genuine pride of patriotism is surely lost when littleness of geographical extent can be construed into a term of reproach. It is the other face of the same vulgarity which boasts that a single British colony is greater than the land which produced Kant and Goethe. " Little Englander " is a name of which no patriot need fear to boast. . . . The use of the term " Little Englander " as a term of scorn does not consist well with a " patriotic " or even an accurate view of our history. It might fairly be asked in reply whether there was nothing to be proud of in " Little England," in her history, her literature, her thought, the great men that she has borne for the world, her struggle for political and religious freedom? The question might be raised whether the British Empire as a whole has any history to show which compares with the history of " Little England "; any science, any literature, any art; or indeed even any great military achievement to be weighed

[1] Mr. Joseph Chamberlain, who was Secretary for the Colonies during the period of the Boer War.

in the scale against the resistance of " Little England "
to Philip II or to Napoleon Buonaparte? [2]

With sufficient knowledge it would be possible to
pass a similar comment upon most of the " little nations " of the world, for the significant personalities
of history have never depended for their influence upon
national power or prestige. Socrates was a citizen of
a Greek city-state; Isaiah belonged to a people who
were no more than a " remnant "; Mohammed came
from an obscure and politically impotent kingdom;
St. Francis, Dante, Savonarola, and Galileo shed luster
upon the name of Italy long before Mussolini sought
to revive the glories of ancient Rome; William Shake-
speare was a son of " little England " when no one
dreamed of a world-wide empire under the Union
Jack; Benjamin Franklin was an American citizen
when the American Republic was little more than an
uncharted wilderness. And so the list could be extended. But no list would be complete without the
greatest of all: for he who is known for all time as the
" Savior of the world " was born in Bethlehem of
Judea when Palestine was merely a petty province under Roman domination. Rome — despite its proud
position as the greatest of " great powers " — crucified
Jesus as an ordinary felon: and the contrast, even from
a nonreligious point of view, is the most tremendous
in human history. On the one side the Emperor in

[2] *Democracy and Reaction*, by L. T. Hobhouse; chapter on " The
Imperial Idea."

his superb palaces, the pomp and power enjoyed by him and his court, the military glory of Rome, the conquered provinces, the long lines of captives, the all-but-invincible legions, the tribute and spoil taken from the whole of the known world. And on the other side — on a hill outside an eastern city in an outlying portion of the Empire — a Man, regarded by the proud Romans as an obscure fanatic, suffering the death of a common malefactor. If the Emperor Tiberius had been told that, so far as he was remembered at all 1900 years later, he would be remembered only with contempt and loathing, but that the memory of his victim in Jerusalem would be revered in tens of thousands of shrines the world over and in regions which Cæsar never knew, he would have dismissed the idea as an impossible delusion. Yet this tremendous fact has come to pass; and in that fact is the final condemnation of the world's distinction between " great powers " and " little nations." For Rome is dead and Jesus lives!

It is clear, therefore, that in the measure that disarmament obliterated this distinction, it would make for a truer sense of human values; and at the same time, by lifting the crushing burden of military preparation, it would release untold capacities of personality of which the world is constantly being robbed today by the prepossessions of armed nationalism.

A second concomitant of disarmament would be a transfer of emphasis from war to law. International relationships would stand on a legal basis, as is the case today in the mutual relationships of states in a federal union; for in a disarmed world, the power to determine the issue of an international dispute could be settled in no other way. Contacts between nations would be on a basis of right instead of might. Moreover, the absence of the power to enforce the claim of one party to a dispute would naturally lead to greater moderation and a more scrupulous regard for justice in the claims presented. Nowadays the " little nation " always stands at a disadvantage in any contest of interest with a " great power," and justice is at the mercy of the nationalistic ambitions of the stronger. The attempt of Nazi Germany to coerce Austria into a political and economic union, or the action of Japan in robbing China of Manchuria, was symptomatic of the nationalist's contempt for the right of smaller or weaker nations; and if in all cases the contempt is not so blatantly or ruthlessly expressed, it is there nevertheless; for there is not a single one of the " great powers " which on occasion has not duplicated the behavior of Germany and Japan. It is this fact, indeed, which made the protest of the great powers in the Manchurian case so ineffective; for — as the Japanese government was quick to point out — so long as they preserve their existing empires (won at the point of the sword and maintained by force) they lay themselves open to a deadly and unanswerable " *tu quoque.*"

This leads on in logical sequence to a third effect of disarmament; for — once the international economy was securely based upon law, and the power to coerce was withdrawn — the relation of imperial powers to their dependencies and colonies would stand upon a basis of trusteeship and co-operation instead of, as at present, a basis of irresponsible control. Lincoln Steffens tells a story in his *Autobiography* which underlines this conclusion and which for that reason is worth repeating. Steffens was in Paris during the Peace Conference in 1919, and states that Clemenceau issued a challenge to his fellows about the conference table. He reports the episode as follows:

The President and the Premiers sat down at the table and were about to proceed to business, while Clemenceau, who was fiddling with his gray silk gloves, said, " One moment, gentlemen. I desire before we go any further to be clear on one very essential point." The President and the Premiers halted and looked up expectantly at Clemenceau, who continued: " I have heard something about a permanent peace. There has been a great deal of talk about a peace to end war for ever, and I am interested in that. But I would like to know whether you mean it, the permanent peace." He looked at his colleagues and they nodded approvingly. " So," Clemenceau said, " you really mean it! Well, it is possible. We can do it; we can make this permanent peace. And we French need, we very much need, the permanent peace. Every time you, our neighbors, get into a fight, France is the battlefield, and our population, our armies, do not increase. If there is not an end of wars we French may all be wiped out some day. So, you see, it is we French more than you remote

Americans, Mr. President, and more than you safe
islanders, Mr. Lloyd George, who require the security
of a real peace. But we French cannot quite believe
you, our friends, neighbors, allies — that you really
mean what you say. Do you, Mr. President?" Mr.
Wilson did. "And you, Mr. Premier?" Mr. Lloyd
George did. And the Italians did, of a certainty, yes.
"Very important," Clemenceau muttered, as if convinced, as if the whole prospect were changing, and
his whole policy. "Very important. We can make this
permanent peace. We can remove all the causes of
war and set up no new causes of war. It is very, very
important what you say, what you have been so long
saying, Mr. President. We here now have the opportunity to make a peace that shall last for ever, and the
diminishing French people will at last be safe. And
you are sure you propose to seize this opportunity?"
They did, they emphatically did intend to seize it.
Clemenceau clucked in his throat; he pressed tight
down the fingers of his glove. "And — you have
counted the costs of such a peace?" The listeners began to grow a little uneasy. Mr. Wilson's eyes became
shifty. Lloyd George twisted in his chair. "What
costs?" "Well," said the realistic Frenchman, "if we
give up all future wars — if we are to prevent war, we
must give up our empires and all hope of empire. You,
Mr. Lloyd George, you English will have to come out
of India, for example; we French will have to come out
of North Africa; and you Americans, Mr. President,
you must get out of the Philippines and Porto Rico and

leave Cuba alone — and Mexico. Oh, we can all go to these countries, but as tourists, traders, travelers; we cannot any more govern them or exploit them or have the inside track in them. We cannot possess the keys to trade routes and spheres of influence. And, yes, we shall have to tear down our tariff walls and open the whole world to free trade and traffic. Those are some of the costs of peace; there are other sacrifices we, the dominant powers, will have to make. It is quite expensive, peace. We French are willing, but are you willing to pay the price of no more war in the world?" The President and the Premiers protested. They did not mean that. They expected to keep their cake and eat it, too. No, no, they did not exactly mean that. "Then," said Clemenceau, sitting up straight and striking the table sharply, "then you don't mean peace. You mean war. And the time for us French to make war is now, when we've got one of our neighbors down; we shall put our foot on him and get ready for — the next war."

An American journalist commenting upon this passage says:

So far as I know, there is no proof that Clemenceau ever said that. The story was never printed in the newspapers. The French reporters said it would be discourteous to print it without American confirmation. But it is none the less a true story, because it tells the truth about peace and about war. It sets forth some of the real causes of war in the modern world. It lays down some of the indispensable requirements of world peace. And, more than these, it exposes some of our pitiful sentimentality in regard to the problem.

It is obviously impossible — in the interests of the many so-called " backward peoples " [3] governed by the British, French, Dutch, and other empires — to suspend imperial rule by a mere stroke of the pen: to do so would not only remove the evils of imperialism but also many of its undoubted benefits. That uncounted benefits have accrued to these peoples under the tutelage of imperial powers is not open to question by anyone who knows the outposts of empire at first hand. Tribal warfare has been eradicated in most cases, sanitation and irrigation have stayed the ravages of plague and famine, roads and railways and other public works have made for intercourse and the growth of trade, the administration of impartial justice has made for security and peace, many ancient superstitions and taboos have been killed, and the natives generally set on the road to a higher standard of living. To that extent, indeed, it is possible to find a certain moral justification for the imperialisms of the nineteenth and twentieth centuries, especially if one fixes upon the beneficent results of this form of government and turns a blind eye upon the admitted barbarity of its methods of conquest.[4] But even if this be acknowledged, such moral

[3] The peoples of India, with their ancient culture and civilization, are of course not included under this designation: the problem of India is in most respects a special one and cannot be covered by any generalizations in regard to imperial rule.

[4] The story of this barbarity can be read in Mr. Winston Churchill's book, *The River War,* or in contemporary accounts of the operations

justification altogether ceased when the League of Nations came into being in 1919. Prior to that date, it was possible to urge with a measure of plausibility that the care and guardianship of " backward races " was the responsibility of the several colonizing powers who, between them, opened up the unexplored portions of the earth and divided them out as imperial domains. However imperfectly that guardianship was exercised, there seemed at the time no alternative which could subdue these uncharted regions to the sway of civilization.

No Christian person, of course, will acknowledge the validity of this dilemma; for from the earliest times the missionary enterprise of the church has known how to improve the lot of " backward peoples " without resort to the violence of imperial conquest: Europe owes the beginnings of its civilization to these missionary methods, and in North America — long before the Red Indians were subdued by white armies — the Jesuits [5] had shown that savages were capable of responding to a Christian approach; and years later, as has already been indicated,[6] William Penn demonstrated the same truth in Pennsylvania. In a sub-Christian world-order, however, which is not prepared

---

against the Matabeles in the 1890's: the methods of Belgian imperialism in subduing the Congo were exposed in 1906 by Mr. E. D. Morel in a book entitled *Red Rubber*.

[5] For the entrancing record of these enterprises the reader is referred to the historical researches of Francis Parkman, especially his *Jesuits in North America* and *The Conspiracy of Pontiac*.

[6] Part I, Chapter VII.

to take the Christian way, the dilemma stands, and on that plane the argument for a beneficent imperialism could not be gainsaid.

But since 1919 the argument no longer holds; for if the care of " backward peoples " is the care of civilization, it is the responsibility of *all* civilized peoples, and not merely of certain self-appointed guardians: and it is precisely for this common responsibility that the Covenant of the League of Nations provides in Article 22. This article has instituted what is known as the "Mandatory System "; and, in the case of the ex-German crown colonies and the ex-Turkish territories in Asia Minor, it provides for the allocation of these areas to certain selected powers who are to act as trustees for the civilized world as represented by the League of Nations. The Mandatory System is not uniform in its application to the territories in question [7] and it needs considerable revision if the principle of trusteeship is to escape the charge of being merely a form of disguised imperialism. But it points the way, in terms of present political reality, whereby imperial control may be robbed of its reproach and become a genuine instrument for what the Covenant calls " the well-being and development of peoples not yet able to stand by themselves under the strenuous conditions of the modern world."

To secure these desirable ends, the Covenant pro-

[7] The Mandates are specified in the Covenant of the League under three divisions, and the conditions governing the Mandates vary according to local conditions; but the general principles are substantially the same in each case.

vides for the maintenance of a permanent "Mandates Commission" to which the several Mandatory Powers shall submit annual reports of their trusteeship. Moreover, in every mandated territory (with certain minor exceptions) it is forbidden to permit any form of forced labor, to conscript the natives for enlistment in the armed forces of the Mandatory, to erect preferential tariffs in favor of the Mandatory, or to exercise discrimination in regard to commercial concessions. It is necessary only to contrast these provisions with prevailing imperial practice to recognize what vast and significant changes the Mandatory System makes. In the Transvaal, the Union of South Africa by the pressure of taxation forces the Kaffir into white employ: in Southwest Africa (under Mandate) she cannot. In Algiers and Tunis, France conscripts natives for the French army: in Syria she is forbidden to do so. In Kenya, Great Britain can penalize the trade of other countries by the imposition of customs duties against non-British goods or give preference to British concessionaires; but in the contiguous territory of Tanganyika such discrimination would be a violation of the Mandate granted by the League of Nations.

The point to notice, however, is that the old type of imperial control maintains itself — whether against rival imperialisms or against native discontent — by means of armaments. This is what is meant when it is said that the British navy is necessary to "defend" a scattered empire: it is required, in other words, to preserve for the British flag territories which other nationalisms may covet and might seize but for the existence of Britain's sea power. Disarmament, therefore, if it stood alone in the world as it is, might easily lead to a fresh scramble among ambitious powers for what the German Emperor once called " a place in the sun."

It is this association of imperialism with armaments which calls for an extension of the Mandatory System as an essential item in the price of world peace. As has been pointed out, the creation of the League of Nations has made the old system of crown colonies and imperial dependencies an anachronism, and has deprived of moral justification every empire based upon armed force; and the logic of the situation, therefore, no less than its ethics, points to the transfer of all the non-self-governing portions of the great empires to the Mandates Commission of the League. This would at once remove one of the most stubborn obstacles to disarmament; for the policy of the " open door " to international commerce, prescribed by the Mandatory System, would cut the nerve of the nationalistic jealousies and resentments aroused today by the " closed door," which makes each empire the exclusive preserve of its own citizens.

It is easy for a British government to disclaim aggressive designs and to acquiesce in the territorial *status quo;* for Great Britain is sated with empire and has no wish for the extension of her imperial responsibilities. But it is not so with most of the land-locked countries of Europe. Their populations are greater in many cases

than that of the British Isles or of France, and many
times the size of imperial Holland or Belgium or
Portugal: yet by the accidents of history they find half
the surface of the globe barred both to their political
ambition and to their administrative capacity. On any
estimate which takes account of moral values, there is
no justice in the present unequal distribution of territory between the five great colonial empires and the
other nations of the world; and the resentment which
ensues is explicable and in most cases justifiable.

Italy and Germany in particular are restive under
this unequal apportionment, and their claim to colonial territory is becoming increasingly a factor in international unrest. It is the old story of those who have
clinging to what they possess, and those who have not
coveting the possessions of others.[8] To concede the
claim to colonies, however, would be no solution to
the problem, for the world is not big enough to satisfy
the " land hunger " of every nation. The only just solution, therefore, lies in the direction indicated above: the
crown colonies and other non-self-governing portions
of the British and every other empire must become
" mandated territories " under the League of Nations.
The ideal arrangement would be the administration of
such territories by an international civil service, freely
open by examination to the nationals of all countries;
but pending such development, the Mandates might

[8] The connection between empire and armaments is well symbolized
in a poster issued by the Navy League of Great Britain, which depicts a
bulldog planted in a menacing attitude upon a recumbent Union Jack and
supported by the motto, " What we have we hold."

well be distributed among such member-states of the
League of Nations as were willing to accept the burden
of trusteeship.   Under such a system the connection
between empire and national armaments would be
broken; for with universal Mandates for "backward
peoples," no one nation would be responsible for the
integrity or defense of colonial areas, but on the contrary they would become the charge of the entire civilized world.

Moreover, the transformation of crown colonies into
mandated territories would have an immediate reaction upon the psychology of subject peoples, and at the
same time it would enable the governing power to dispense with a large measure of the armed force which
is now deemed necessary for the discharge of imperial
oversight.   Under an empire, subject peoples have no
remedy for grievances except appeal to the government
which inflicts the grievances, or in the last resort rebellion.   The natives of Kenya, for instance, may and do
object to the redistribution of the Kavirondo reserves
in the interests of gold-mining companies; but their sole
court of appeal is the Colonial Office in London.[9]   Under a Mandatory System, however, they would have a
right of appeal from London, where they are not represented, to Geneva, where their interests are safe-
guarded by the Commission of the League.   There is
every reason to believe that even the complex and diffi-

[9] This is strictly true only of non-justiciable disputes: questions of law
can of course be carried by native representatives to the Privy Council; but
it is the former which constitute the main grievances of subject peoples,
and in regard to these no appeal is possible under imperial control.

cult problem of India would yield a solution if the good offices of the League of Nations were substituted for the sole efforts of the British Raj, however sincere and disinterested those efforts may be. Indeed, some such course would be inevitable if disarmament made the continued military domination of India impossible.

Whether that is so or not, however, it is clear that in a disarmed world the absence of the power to coerce would necessitate a reconstitution of the existing relationship between imperial powers and their colonial dependencies; and this change must therefore be envisaged by all who contemplate the abolition of war and the building of world peace upon secure foundations.

There is one other change associated with disarmament which must be considered by those who are prepared to pay the price of peace. Armaments — whether they be armies or navies or air forces — are useless apart from the bases from which they operate. It is this which explains the tenacity with which a naval power like Great Britain clings to the multitude of strategic points and waterways over which her flag flies; for these strategic points control the sea-borne commerce of the world, and the armed power, therefore, which holds them is able in time of war to strangle the international trade of the enemy and to restrict the movements of his navy. To travel by way of Suez to the Orient is to realize that the world's shipping sails the high seas only by permission of John Bull. Gibraltar, Malta, Port Said, Suez, Aden, Colombo, Singapore, Hong Kong — these form a chain of fortifications which could at any moment deny the freedom of the seas to all vessels not under the British flag. The peace-loving Briton knows that such action would never be undertaken except under some dire national distress; but the citizen of other nations is apt to see in this string of bases an insolent assertion of arbitrary power, which denies to him the freedom which the Briton claims for himself. Obviously, then, the political status of these points cannot be dissociated from the question of disarmament; for whoever controls them is in a position of strategic advantage which excites the fear of other nations and makes them unwilling to disarm.

How, then, should they be treated? It is no solution to hand them back (as is sometimes suggested) to the nations from which they were originally torn; for international gateways are an international concern; and in this respect, as in others, nationalism must yield to the interests of humanity if world peace is to be preserved. There is only one solution in harmony with these interests: as with crown colonies, strategic points must be internationalized by transferring them to the sovereignty of the League of Nations. Yet the Mandatory System does not apply here; for as a rule in these fortified ports there are no large native populations whose interests need to be conserved: their only function is to supply fuel and dock facilities for ships, landing places for aeroplanes, and dumps for munitions; and as such their control by a Mandatory would be open to all the objections which attach to their present status. In one of President Wilson's famous " Fourteen Points," which he laid down as conditions of peace with Germany in 1918, he insisted upon " the freedom of the seas in peace and in war, except in so far as they shall be closed by international action." That was before the days of the League of Nations; but it indicates the only condition upon which the world's strategic points and waterways can become an asset and not a threat to the peace of the world; and the only effective method of fulfilling that condition is to vest the control of all such points [10] in an international commission which shall act not for one nation but for all. Such a step will not be taken without a deep wound to nationalistic pride, for it means a reversal of time-honored policies; but without it disarmament and world peace will continue to elude the efforts of idealists and realists alike.

To sum up. The problem of world peace can be approached either from the side of disarmament or from the side of national policy: for each reacts upon the other. The advocacy of disarmament must go hand in hand with a peaceable foreign policy, and this implies the willing acceptance of changes which often cut sharply across the sentiments of nationalism. On the other hand, to adopt policies which take account of the rights and needs of other nations, and which therefore require no armed defense, is to engender an international feeling in which disarmament becomes practical politics.

[10] This of course would apply to the western hemisphere no less than to the eastern, and include the Panama Zone as well as the Suez Canal.

CHAPTER XVI

THE SANCTIONS OF INTERNATIONAL PEACE

AN INCREASING number of people see that the choice to-day is between international anarchy on the one hand (in which each nation is " sovereign " and uncontrolled), and on the other an international order (in which nations are controlled by a federal authority as the citizen is controlled by the authority of the state). The first-named condition — as all history conclusively demonstrates — means periodic war, while the last-named implies the reign of law. If this analogy is pressed it seems to point to what is called an International Police Force as the sanction behind international law. The argument is as follows:

In any organized society the liberty of the individual to do as he likes is checked and qualified by social regulations and statutes; and if he offends against these and asserts his personal " sovereignty " in defiance of the reign of law, he is dealt with by the police whose business it is to arrest the wrongdoer and hale him before a court of law, which then passes judgment upon his case and either acquits him or punishes him according to his deserts. It should be the same (so it is argued) with the society of nations as with a society of individuals; and consequently the logical corollary of a League of Nations, or of any other international organization, is an International Police Force which can be set in motion against a recalcitrant state alleged to be guilty of breaking international law. Sir Norman Angell, with his usual genius for clarity of statement, has put the argument thus: "We should all like to see armed force eliminated from human intercourse, but since this cannot be in the world as it is, it is better to place force behind international law than to leave it in the hands of national ligitants."[1] It is to be observed that the function of an International Police Force is not to coerce the alleged wrongdoer into submitting to the will of the League of Nations, but only to compel him to submit his case to adjudication, so that justice may be done between him and the others. One frequently hears the plea that a nation's army or navy is its policeman, and that armies and navies exist for the same reason that the police force exists. But there is a cardinal difference between the two institutions. Police forces are not organized to fight each other, and armies are; moreover, armies are forces behind rival litigants, while the police constitute a force behind the judge. In other words, the police method makes the defense of the individual the obligation of society, while, contrariwise, the military method, as it now exists, rejects the principle of social defense in favor of each unit defending himself. The one is a social instrument, the other an

---

[1] I have summarized in the following sentences the cogent argument which Sir Norman Angell develops in his book, *The Unseen Assassins:* see especially Chapter VI, on " The Sovereign Assassin."

instrument of anarchy; the one depends upon competition of power, each seeking to be stronger than the other (which is mathematically impossible); the other depends upon the pooling of individual power, so that by the co-operation of all the rights of each may be maintained. The two methods are plainly antagonistic and mutually exclusive in their aims.

It may be admitted at once that to place an International Police Force at the disposal of the League of Nations (were such a step politically feasible) would be an immense advance upon the present international system, or want of system, which allows competing national sovereignties to act on the principle that might is right, and which in the final resort seeks to establish international justice by the clash of armed force. The proposal has been described as "putting teeth into the Covenant of the League," and in the prevailing state of world opinion (which is not yet prepared to renounce the use of force), the erection of some system of armed sanctions for the maintenance of peace may be the next step in the evolution of international relationships toward world order. Nations can and will act only in accordance with the moral standards which are generally accepted by their citizens, and it is not, therefore, to discredit the attempt to eliminate violence from civilized intercourse to say that concentration of armed force in the hands of a centralized authority would be a sign of steady advance, on the part of the world at large, from chaotic barbarism to civilized order.

It is sometimes urged that a civilized international

order is impossible by reason of the natural pugnacity
of human nature; it is often deemed a sufficient refuta-
tion of the case for organized peace to say that " there
always have been wars and there always will be wars."
Yet in reality the antisocial instincts of the ordinary
man are an argument *for* the League of Nations, not
against it. If the world's population consisted entirely
of wholly Christian people bent upon the will of God
as their supreme obligation, an International Police
Force — indeed even our civil police — would never be
needed for anything more than point-duty or to advise
well-intentioned citizens of the best way to go about
their business. It is precisely because human nature is
not fully Christianized, because it is liable to gusts of
passion and unreason, in a word, because man is — on
one side of his being — a fighting animal, that the re-
straining hand of the police is necessary in order that
human disputes may be settled by process of law, and
in order to prevent the resulting anarchy which would
follow if each citizen were responsible for the defense
of his own rights. No one in his senses suggests that
the barons of England should organize (as once they
did) local armies for the maintenance of their baronial
or territorial privileges; yet a precisely similar absurdity
is accepted when law-abiding citizens endorse the ex-
travagance of national armaments and decry any effort
to subordinate national sovereignty to the collective
authority and power of a League of Nations.

The case for an International Police Force having
been stated (though not necessarily endorsed in every

particular), it is necessary to scrutinize the idea of armed sanctions from a practical point of view, and also in the light of Christian principle.

On the practical side, it is important not to be misled by the term "Police." In *function* an international force might fill the role of a policeman, in the sense that its sole purpose would be to defend the common peace and to bring an aggressor-nation to justice; but in *method* what is proposed is not police action but military action; for it is physically impossible to hale a whole people before a court of law, and even its rulers or representatives could not be arrested without an armed invasion which would immediately precipitate a state of war. For the effective discharge of the police function, therefore, two preliminary conditions are necessary.[2] One is a Disarmament Convention by which the signatory nations (which for this purpose must include all nations) agree to discard all weapons of an aggressive character, retaining only defensive weapons and such equipment as is necessary to maintain civil order in time of domestic crisis. And the other is a monopoly by the International Force of the weapons which the several nations discard: tanks, heavy artillery, warplanes and poison gas would then be concentrated solely in the hands of the League of Nations, and as such would constitute the policeman's baton of the International Authority.

---

[2] The practical problems connected with an International Police Force have been exhaustively worked out by Lord Davies in his book, *The Problem of the Twentieth Century:* see especially Chapter X.

In passing, it may be noted that the existing sanctions at the disposal of the League of Nations are inoperative precisely because these two conditions are not contemplated. Article 16 of the League Covenant provides in the last resort for a League "Police," which is to consist of quotas of armed force contributed by the several states-members of the League. But the preliminary condition of national disarmament is not included; and it is obvious, therefore, that any attempt to invoke Article 16 would at once issue in a first-class war between the League powers on the one side and the recalcitrant nation and his allies on the other.[3] A further obstacle to the operation of Article 16 lies in the fact that at present the League does not include certain major powers,[4] and League action therefore would not command unanimous support against an aggressor.

Assuming, however, that these defects were remedied, and assuming also that the two conditions named above were duly fulfilled, despite the technical difficulties involved,[5] what would be the situation from a practical point of view? It is obvious that the constitution of an International Police Force could not be carried

[3] It was this difficulty which prevented the application of sanctions to the Græco-Italian dispute in 1923 and to the Sino-Japanese conflict in 1932: Italy and Japan were respectively adjudged guilty of aggression, but the League could not implement its condemnation without resort to war.

[4] The United States, Japan and Germany.

[5] How is an International Force to be recruited? by whom trained and commanded? upon what centers would it be based? where would its aerodromes be located? Lord Davies, in *The Problem of the Twentieth Century*, faces all these questions, and shows that the technical difficulties are not an insuperable barrier.

through unless we presuppose the overwhelming support of public opinion in every country in the world. Indeed, in the final issue, the civil police everywhere depend upon the same support for their effectiveness. Where — as in Ireland in 1921 before the grant of dominion status — this support was lacking, the police were impotent and the authority of the courts could not be maintained, even with all the weight of the British army behind them. The same was true of the federal police in the United States, in their efforts to enforce prohibition against the rising tide of public objection. But where public opinion is on the side of the police and against the lawbreaker, the police rarely if ever need to invoke the use of force. The remarkable and oft-remarked efficiency of the unarmed London policeman is due to this fact.

It is therefore legitimate to assume that the same principle would operate in the case of an International Police Force. Without a common international agreement to institute such a force it could never come into being, and much less exercise its power. But once such agreement was secured, its armed power would never be used; for the pressure of world opinion would be in itself a " sanction " which the most determined aggressor would not dare to defy and which, in any case in a disarmed world, he would not have the power to resist.

Even if it were not so, however, it is not necessary to assume that armed force in the form of air raids and poison gas and other military abominations would necessarily be called into play. For military operations need only be a last and desperate resort at the very end of a graduated scale of pressure. The international authority, in the absence of national armaments, would have a variety of weapons at its disposal, apart altogether from any military equipment with which it might be endowed. These could include the refusal of passports to the citizens of the offending nation, an embargo on credits and arms (so as to prevent rearmament), and the severance of diplomatic relations. If these were not sufficient to restrain the unsocial action of the aggressor, an economic boycott could be instituted which would cut off his imports and exports (except for necessary foodstuffs, which on humanitarian grounds should be allowed to enter). No blockade of a naval or military kind would be necessary, for all that would be required would be a refusal to accept the aggressor's goods: under the conditions of international trade such a refusal would automatically stop the flow of imports to the aggressor, since without either exports or credits he would be unable to purchase the goods he required.[6] It is only if and when these and similar measures had failed to secure the submission of the dispute to adjudication, that the International Police Force would be called upon to subject certain selected spots of commercial or political importance to bombardment. Moreover, since it alone would possess aggressive weapons it would be in no danger of counterattack, and it could therefore give due warning of bom-

---

[6] There is no need to justify these statements, for they belong to the A B C of political economy.

bardment and allow sufficient time to elapse for the removal of the population from the danger zones.[7] The military action of an International Police Force would thus destroy property but not life. As a final measure, a provisional government under international authority might take over the administration of the aggressor-state until such time as the dispute had been adjudicated and the judgment accepted.

Under existing conditions of armed national sovereignty, such drastic measures would, of course, be impossible of execution; but if we postulate, as is necessary, a world opinion which has already agreed to the disarming of the several nations and the clothing of an international authority with executive powers, the situation envisaged differs in no fundamental respect from the action which could be taken — in case of need — by a federal government against a rebellious province.

It is, indeed, to the analogy of a political federation rather than to the existence of a civil police force that we ought to turn, if we would understand the " sanctions of international peace." During the first 150 years' history of the United States there were thirty-nine cases of interstate dispute brought before the Supreme Court at Washington; and of this class of case it is reported that " no State of the American Union has ever refused to comply with and obey the decision of the Supreme Court." [8] In no case has it been necessary to resort even

[7] This is the actual technique which is frequently employed today in so-called " police action " against border tribes.

[8] *The Supreme Court and Sovereign States,* by C. Warren, quoted by Lord Davies in *The Problem of the Twentieth Century,* p. 707.

to the mildest form of coercion for the enforcement of the Court's decision: on only two occasions has even a threat of coercion been necessary,[9] and in both cases the threat was sufficient to induce compliance with the judgment, since public opinion was behind the Supreme Court and the resisting states had no armaments with which to contest the federal authority. Objection has several times been taken to the Court's judgment by states concerned;[10] in no single instance, however, has the objection been carried to the point of rebellion. Commenting on this fact an eminent legal writer says: "There has hitherto been no instance in our judicial annals of the enforcement of a judgment against a state."[11]

It will be observed that we have in this record of the United States Supreme Court an exact illustration of those two conditions which have been indicated as necessary for the successful and bloodless operation of an International Police Force; namely, states without "offensive" armaments, and the concentration of superior power in the hands of the federal authority. And in both respects the conditions had the backing of public opinion, and were therefore effective in preserving the peaceful organization of the United States without recourse to coercion. The American Civil

[9] Both of them in 1832, against Georgia over a private suit, and against South Carolina in regard to tariffs.

[10] The case of Ohio in 1864 and of West Virginia in 1915 are the best known.

[11] *Judicial Settlement of Controversies between States,* by J. B. Scott, Solicitor for the Department of State in Washington; quoted by Lord Davies, in *The Problem of the Twentieth Century,* p. 710.

War points the same moral. For — though hostilities were not in defiance of any ruling of the Supreme Court — they could not have occurred had it not been for the fact that, prior to the war, the federal authority had weakly permitted the accumulation of "offensive" weapons by the confederate states.

The problem, therefore, which would confront an International Police Force is not the task of waging war against a recalcitrant nation-state, but the lesser and easier task of preventing its rearmament and inducing it to submit its case to the arbitrament of law. In the light of a century and a half's experience in the United States, it is well within the probabilities to affirm that these tasks could be performed without resorting to any other weapon than the force of world opinion.

It remains now to examine the idea of an International Police Force in the light of Christian principle, and to ask whether or not Christian people contribute to world peace by its advocacy and support. This question has already been touched upon in the Preface to this book (to which reference should be made at this point); but one or two further considerations may be mentioned.

In so far as an International Police Force engaged in actual battle, its organization and activity would be open to all the moral objections which can be leveled against war, and it is not possible therefore to contemplate a Christian's participation in military operations by an international force without disloyalty to his faith. The devilry of war is not sanctified just because it is waged in the name of the League of Nations; for the Christian objection to war is not to its aim (if that aim is just, as it may conceivably be), but to its methods, which are of necessity a contradiction of all that is meant by a Christian life. The Christian gospel indicates another and a better way of dealing with aggressive evil than the use of the sword; and the Christian therefore makes his most effective contribution to peace when he remains true to his faith, and seeks to implement it by Christianizing his nation's policy.

For himself, the Christian pacifist is prepared to take the risks of an unarmed international order, and to repudiate the way of war in any circumstances. But a world that is not fully Christianized will necessarily live on a sub-Christian level; and all therefore that the Christian has a right to ask from such a world is that it shall be true to the standards and methods to which it already consents. At the same time he will urge it, by every means within his power, to move persistently and progressively in the direction of the Christian ideal; and one way — indeed the only finally effective way — of doing this is for the Christian himself to show, by the fidelity of his own life and conduct, what the Christian ideal means and what it requires of those who are faithful to it.

The Christian, therefore, who is persuaded of the essential iniquity of war cannot himself enlist in an International Police Force, equipped for military operations. But there is no moral inconsistency in associating this refusal with a recognition of the fact that the organization of an International Police Force, under a world authority, would be a striking and significant step toward the realization of a Christian world order. The Christian citizen supports the organization of law within the social order, without thereby approving all the practices and institutions of national life; he accepts courts of law, for instance, even though they resort on occasion to capital punishment. In a similar way, therefore, he could, without a denial of his faith, support and encourage an international order, even though it were associated with armed sanctions; for the very agreement to pool these sanctions would tend to cancel out the rival nationalisms which are so prolific a source of world disorder. It is by no means certain (the probabilities are in the other direction, as stated above) that the military power of an International Police Force would ever be called into action. For that reason it may rightly be claimed that an International Police Force in the hands of a League of Nations would register a move away from war and in the direction of law; and, increasingly, international consent and co-operation would take the place of international coercion and conflict.

CHAPTER XVII

THE ASSENT OF PUBLIC OPINION TO THE CHRISTIAN IDEAL OF WORLD PEACE

THE foregoing chapters of this book have endeavored to show that the chief enemy of the Christian ideal of world peace is nationalism, and that war under modern conditions means the suicide of humanity. The obvious alternative to nationalism is internationalism, on lines already drawn (though not completed) by the League of Nations. But this involves changes in national policy and qualifications of state sovereignty which cut sharply across prevailing traditions, deeply rooted in human habit and historic sentiment: and it is these traditions of nationalism which prevent the organization of the world in terms of collective rather than national responsibility for peace and orderly intercourse between peoples. The creation of an International Police Force might ensure this orderly intercourse; but its power would lie not so much in the armed sanctions at its disposal as in the public opinion by which it was directed and upheld.

The Christian's contribution to world peace, therefore, turns in the last analysis upon his ability to win public opinion to his side, and to secure popular support for the changes in national status which are the necessary price of peace. Unless this can be done, and unless the emotions of nationalism can be transferred to the ideals of internationalism, the world will sink into chaos under the impact of war, and civilization will break into fragments.

Consequently it is vitally important to ask how the assent of public opinion is to be enlisted on behalf of internationalism. For, if once we could establish a widespread conviction that war is outside the conventions of decent society, public opinion would be proof against war scares, however stimulated, and even the sinister machinations of armament firms would not avail to set people against people. Statesmen therefore would be compelled to compose international differences by some other method than an appeal to arms.

The cynic regards this as an impossible dream, and his argument is familiar to everyone who pleads for world peace: usually it consists in the reiterated statement that " you cannot change human nature." The Christian faith rests upon the conviction that, under the power of the gospel, human nature *can* be changed: selfish men can become unselfish, the morally timid can become morally courageous, those who are apathetic to spiritual values can be charged with enthusiasm, vice can be transformed into virtue, sinners can become saints. But even when human nature is not subjected to this radical conversion, it is not open to doubt that if " you cannot change human nature," it is possible to change human behavior. This indeed is the explanation of man's emergence from barbarism into civilization. In western Europe and America, for instance, we no longer indulge in infanticide or the burning of witches; we do not beat tom-toms to scare away an eclipse of the sun; we do not take " a hair of the dog that bit us " to ward off hydrophobia; nor do surgeons " bleed " their patients as a cure for common ailments. In a multitude of ways human behavior has adjusted itself to new knowledge and new habits; and in no respect is this more complete than in regard to the " fighting instinct " which the cynic holds to be ineradicable. Little more than a hundred years ago the duel was a commonly accepted institution in polite society, and no man of honor would refuse a challenge. The infant American Republic was robbed of her most constructive statesman when Aaron Burr killed Alexander Hamilton in a duel in 1804; in 1809 George Canning (who was Secretary for Foreign Affairs in the British Government) fought with and was wounded by Lord Castlereagh (who was Secretary for War), as a result of a political disagreement; and as late as 1829 the Duke of Wellington exchanged shots with a fellow member of the House of Lords. There were cynics in those days, as in these, who regarded the duel as an inevitable outcome of human nature: yet within half a century human behavior had changed, and the institution of dueling had disappeared from the English-speaking world.[1] It is not that the personal issues which led to the duel have ceased to vex human relationships: the change in behavior is due to the fact

[1] Dueling was made illegal in England in 1844.

that public opinion now regards civil society as the guardian of personal honor and private right, and the habit has therefore been established of settling disputes between individuals by process of law instead of by a species of war.

The disappearance of dueling underlines the problem which confronts every advocate of world peace: How can we create in the public at large a state of mind which will prefer internationalism to nationalism and so make war as impossible as dueling?

The usual answer to this question is in the word "propaganda"; and it would be foolish not to recognize how great is the need among all classes of the community for a persistent and systematic presentation of the case for international authority and world peace. This is the function especially of the schools, the universities and the churches; for by the very terms of their existence they are pledged to propagate a culture of mind and spirit which is wider than mere nationalism. But this needs to be supplemented by the efforts of those who undertake — through the printed and spoken word — definitely to educate the public mind on questions like disarmament, the League of Nations, and world peace generally. In this respect the Christian citizen has a specific contribution to make; for unless good sense be supplemented by good will, all the education in the world will not cure the ills of a planet equipped for war. Without the moral appeal, therefore, propaganda for peace will not carry the day; for when the passions of nationalism are aroused men will do things which are against reason, against their economic interest, even against the very nation they profess to serve. Only an opposing passion — devotion to something wider than nationalism — can offset these baser passions; and it is this which Christianity engenders when it calls men and women to the obedience of Christian discipleship.

One illustration may be permitted in this connection. Reference has been made [2] to the horrors of modern warfare, and it has been pointed out that the appeal to horror is apt to defeat its own ends by inducing fear. But here it is that the Christian impulse acts as a corrective; for it provokes the question, not " Can I *endure* the horrors of war? " but, " Ought I to *inflict* the horrors of war? " It turns a physical problem into a moral problem. Mr. John Galsworthy, shortly before he died, indicated this problem in a letter to the Disarmament Conference which assembled in Geneva in 1932:

When a child is outraged or done to death in time of peace, the whole nation is stirred. In wartime, millions of children are outraged and done to death, in manner not the same, but as horrible. On them are forced slow starvation, illness, deformities, orphanage, death from disease, gas and bombs. . . . Let those men therefore who will soon meet for the avowed purpose of considering how far they can minimize the chances and the scope of war put, each one to himself, this

[2] Chapter V.

question: If I were incited to outrage and murder a child, what should I say and do to him who incited me? And let them remember that, however far from their thoughts it be that children should suffer, war will inevitably outrage and destroy them.[3]

The Christian answer to this question is not in doubt; for when we turn to the Founder of the Faith from whom all Christian inspiration comes, it is obvious that he *endured* even the appalling horror of the cross with unbroken fidelity to the will of God; but in fidelity to that same will, he renounced the sword and refused to *inflict* even the minor horror of a severed ear. The Christian therefore makes his specific contribution to peace only when he associates propaganda with the spirit and outlook of Jesus Christ; for such propaganda must have as its final aim, not merely the apprehension of facts, but the creation of a state of mind which has a passion for human fellowship, and which therefore is proof against the divisive passion of nationalism.

Propaganda, however, presumes the existence of receptive minds, willing to listen and ready to be persuaded. But that is a presumption which applies only to a small section of the population of every country; and meantime the mass of the people are still held by the traditions of nationalism, and are impervious to — because untouched by — an enlightening propaganda.

[3] The full text of the letter appears in *John Galsworthy*, by Herman Ould.

At any moment, therefore, they are liable to be stampeded into a warlike temper and warlike demands by gusts of fear or hate or national pride. A signal instance of this kind of reaction occurred in 1898, when American nationalism was fanned into flame by the sinking of the United States warship "Maine" in Havana harbor. No proof has ever been offered that the Spanish authorities were guilty; and it was clearly a case for judicial investigation by an international tribunal; but President McKinley was pushed into war with Spain by the frenzied insistence of Congress, and he allowed his better judgment to go by default. A similar reaction was produced in England in 1899, when interests bent upon the annexation of the Transvaal and its gold fields played upon nationalistic feeling by false and plausible stories of the "danger to British women and children" under the Boer regime. These two instances are typical of the public reaction under the prevailing order of armed and rival nationalisms; and they emphasize the necessity of reaching the popular mind by some other technique than that of reasoned propaganda.

Fortunately, that other technique lies ready to hand in what may be called the pressure of political fact. It consists in establishing, in times of public indifference and by the conscious forethought of idealists, conditions which will become part of the accepted tradition of national life, and which therefore in times of national excitement will — by the very inertia of tradition — assist the maintenance of peace. The meaning of this technique can best be made clear by a series of illustrations.

We see its operation, for instance, in civil life when we consider the elimination of dueling. As long ago as the early seventeenth century Francis Bacon condemned the duel as " a direct affront of law "; and he was followed in his condemnation by lawyers and divines through the two succeeding centuries. But, as already indicated, dueling disappeared from English life only when the civil courts could be relied upon to administer impartial justice, and when, therefore, recourse to law became a normal habit of the people generally. In that way a new tradition was created, under which the duel became a thing of disrepute rather than of honor; and finally the new tradition was incorporated in an Act of Parliament supported by public opinion. The idealists who fought for clean justice created a new social fact, and the pressure of that fact killed the institution of dueling.

The same technique may be observed in international life. After the war of 1812–14 between Great Britain and the United States (during which Canada had been invaded and the city of Washington burned by the contending armies), two farseeing men, anxious to prevent a repetition of such calamities and the ill will which they breed, drafted a scheme for the perpetual disarmament of the Great Lakes and the land frontier between the two countries. The inspiration to this achievement came from Richard Rush, a Philadelphia Quaker, and he found a ready collaborator in Sir Charles Bagot, the

British Ambassador in Washington. The people on either side of the frontier were war-weary and entirely indifferent to high politics; and it was this which gave to these two idealists for peace their unique opportunity. The treaty (known to history as the Rush-Bagot Agreement of 1817) was accepted by both countries without objection, and with little public notice. But once in operation it began to establish a new tradition; and today that tradition, with over a hundred years of peace behind it, has made the very thought of war between the United States and Canada an outrage to the sentiments of both people. Neither country arms against the other, for a state of mind has been created, north and south of the international line, which has already withstood the shock of half a dozen crises since 1817, and which now makes the Canadian-American border the safest frontier in the world. An imposing memorial to the work of Richard Rush and Sir Charles Bagot has been built by the American and Canadian governments [4] on the site of Fort Niagara: and it stands as a significant reminder of the technique by which the pressure of political fact has implemented the dreams of the idealists into the fabric of an enduring peace. The then President of the United States, in a speech on Canadian soil in 1923, drew attention to that fact in words which deserve a wide publicity: the words are carved in granite upon a monument in Stanley Park, Vancouver, erected on the spot where the President

---

[4] The memorial was formally dedicated by public ceremonial on September 3, 1934.

spoke. "What an object-lesson of Peace," he said, " is shown today by our two countries to all the world. No grim-faced fortifications mark our frontiers; no huge battleships patrol our dividing waters; no stealthy spies lurk in our border hamlets. Only a scrap of paper recording hardly more than a simple understanding safeguards lives and properties on the Great Lakes, and only humble mileposts mark the inviolable boundary-line for thousands of miles through farm and forest. Our protection is in our fraternity, our armor is our faith, the tie that binds more firmly year by year is ever-increasing acquaintance and comradeship through interchange of citizens; and the compact is not of perishable parchment, but of fair and honorable dealing which God grant shall continue for all time."

The significance of these illustrations cannot be too highly stressed, for they point the way by which conscious propaganda for peace may be silently reinforced by the unconscious pressure of political fact, until the very indifference of the multitude — which so often baffles the idealist — may become his greatest asset. The League of Nations and the Pact of Paris for the outlawry of war [5] have considerably more hold upon public esteem today than had the Rush-Bagot Agreement one hundred years ago; and the task of the peace advocate, therefore, is to induce statesmen to support and invoke these instruments, in season and out of

[5] The signatories of the Pact of Paris, who include every nation in the world, are pledged never to resort to war as " an instrument of national policy."

season, until precedents are established, and the people become habituated to the subordination of nationalism to internationalism.

There have been important occasions in quite recent years when this technique might have been adopted in Great Britain. In 1928, for instance, fifty-four nations signed the Pact of Paris, by which they solemnly agreed to adopt peaceful means in all international disputes. But the British government inserted a reservation in its acceptance of the Pact, whereby Great Britain's signature is given " on the distinct understanding that it does not prejudice her freedom of action in respect of certain regions which constitute a special and vital interest for the Empire's peace and safety." [6]

A similar reservation was appended to the British signature of the Optional Clause, in 1930, by which it was agreed to submit all international disputes to arbitration. Countries like Egypt, Iraq and Afghanistan are therefore specifically ruled out from this peaceable treatment in case of clash with Great Britain.

It was by virtue of this reservation that, in 1932, the Dominions Office in London, in the dispute with the Irish Free State over land annuities, refused the Free State's request to submit the case to the League's adjudication before the World Court. In other words, British Imperial affairs were treated as the sole concern of the British Empire, and the League therefore must not be allowed to interfere!

Legally the British government was within its rights,

[6] *British Note to the United States,* May 19, 1928.

but nevertheless excellent opportunities were missed for enhancing the prestige of the League; for the public indifference was such that it would have roused little interest and no resentment if the Pact of Paris and the Optional Clause had been accepted without reservations, or if the League had been invited to assist in securing a settlement of the Irish issue. On the other hand, the very indifference of the public could have been used in the interests of world peace; for a willingness to use the League and a readiness to waive technical rights would have strengthened the habit of internationalism and made the League's intermediation more readily acceptable in a crisis. It is difficult to take seriously the encomiums which statesmen pass upon the League of Nations, when those same statesmen refuse their consent to international action which conflicts with the traditional prerogatives of national sovereignty.

The time to establish the precedents which make for peace is not when a crisis inflames public feeling, but when the apathy of the populace can be counted upon to raise no objection. There are many ways in which this can be done. Proposals, for instance, have been made for the passage of peace legislation by all governments signatory to the League of Nations. The new Spanish Republic has already embodied such legislation in its national constitution; and the British Labor party, in its official statement of foreign policy, has announced its intention of securing as soon as possible a Peace Act of Parliament. This Act would bring national legislation into full accord with the international obligations which Great Britain has already accepted under the Covenant of the League and the various agreements for consultation and arbitration: these obligations would be duly set forth in the schedule of the Act, and British subjects — soldiers and civilians alike — would be legally relieved of obedience to any national order or regulation, or to any military command, which conflicted with these wider obligations. The mere existence of such an Act of Parliament would put a restraint upon jingo statesmanship, and it would engender a state of mind which would make a call to arms fall upon deaf ears, and which automatically, if a crisis arose, would prefer law to war.

In ways of that kind, therefore, the peace advocate can bring the pressure of political fact to bear upon popular indifference; and so, with ever increasing effect, secure the assent of public opinion to the maintenance of international peace.

It is no light or easy task which confronts the peace advocate; for the traditions of nationalism are deeply rooted in human feeling the world over; and the protagonist of internationalism therefore may easily yield to despair. But just here the Christian citizen can make his most fundamental contribution to peace. For in all the concerns of life he is upheld by a triumphant faith. He sees the way of God in Jesus Christ; and therefore he believes that the Christian ideal of world peace has the backing of the moral order of the universe: for him, eternal reality is on the side of world fellowship; and for that reason there is warrant for hope and for perseverance. Mr. Bernard Shaw, in the Preface to *On the Rocks,* has struck this note in a dialogue between Jesus and Pilate. Jesus speaks as follows to the Roman governor:

Speak no more vain things to me about the greatness of Rome. The greatness of Rome, as you call it, is nothing but fear; fear of the past and fear of the future; fear of the poor; fear of the rich; . . . fear of the High Priests; fear of the Jews and Greeks who are learned; fear of the Gauls and Goths and Huns who are barbarians; fear of the Carthage you destroyed to save you from the fear of it, and which now you fear more than ever; fear of Imperial Cæsar, the idol you have yourself created; and fear of me, the penniless vagrant, buffeted and mocked; fear of everything except the rule of God; faith in nothing but blood and iron and gold. You, standing for Rome, are the universal coward; and I, standing for the Kingdom of God, have braved everything, lost everything, and won an eternal crown.

It is this faith which makes the difference between the world's way and the Christian way. Despair of the Christian ideal is always atheistic; for it leaves God out of account and treats the problem of world peace as a mere conflict of human wills. But, as William Lloyd Garrison once put it, " God and one make a majority "; and, inspired by that faith, the Christian can stand for peace, in the conviction that he stands on the winning side.

INDEX